Beyond the Classroom
Exploring Active Citizenship
in 11-16 Education

Beyond the Classroom
Exploring Active Citizenship in 11-16 Education
Edited by Benjamin Linsley & Elisabeth Rayment

Published by The New Politics Network January 2004

Design and layout: Benjamin Linsley
Cover image: Getty Images
Additional material: Elisabeth Rayment, Peter Facey & Benjamin Linsley
Printed: Halstan & Co. Ltd., Amersham, Bucks, HP6 6HJ
Distributed: Warnes Mail Marketing Ltd, London

ISBN 0 9545982 0 2

The New Politics Network is a not for profit, independent, political and campaigning think tank, concerned with issues relating to democratic renewal and popular participation in politics. We work with all political parties as well as a wide range of groups and individuals to provide an independent and innovative debate on the future of politics.

The New Politics Network
6 Cynthia Street
London N1 9JF

Tel: 020 7278 4443   Fax: 020 7278 4425   Email: info@new-politics.net
www.new-politics.net

Acknowledgements:
The Network would like to express its sincerest thanks to:
Sir Bernard Crick, Tony Breslin, John Potter, Prof. Priscilla Alderson, Derry Hannam, Jeremy Cunningham, Dr Liam Gearon, Bill Freeman, Sally Stenton, Carrie Supple, Sheila Bloom, Liz Byrne, Matt Henn, Mark Weinstein, Martin Bratt and Matthew Green MP
Additional thanks go to:
Peter Pattison, Stephen Twigg MP, Dr Howard Williamson
Suzanne Samson, Emily Robinson & Aglaya Snetkov

The opinions in this paper reflect those of the individual authors only.

Contents

Contents

Contributors

Sir Bernard Crick is Emeritus Professor of Politics at Birkbeck College, University of London. He was chairman and main draftsman of the 1998 report *Education for Citizenship and the Teaching of Democracy in Schools* and adviser on citizenship to the DfES 1998-2000, subsequently appointed by the Home Secretary as chair of the 'Life in the United Kingdom' Advisory Group whose report *The New and the Old* appeared last September on education for naturalisation. His main books have been *In Defence of Politics* (1962); *George Orwell: a Life* (1981), and more recently *Essays on Citizenship* (2000) and *Crossing Borders* (2003).

Tony Breslin prior to his appointment as Chief Executive of the Citizenship Foundation, was General Adviser (14-19 Education) in the London Borough of Enfield where his work brought together issues around Sixth Form funding, the various aspects of Curriculum 2000, the Key Skills and Citizenship agendas and the development of lifelong learning provision. Prior to his appointment in Enfield he taught and held senior and middle management positions at comprehensive schools in Haringey and Hertfordshire.

John Potter is an independent educational consultant and author. Formerly the Director of Curriculum Resources at CSV, he is the author of *Active Citizenship in Schools: a good practice guide to developing a whole school policy.* He is currently working with Titus Alexander on *The Future of Schools*; more details are available at www.transformingschools.org.uk.

Professor Priscilla Alderson is Professor of Childhood Studies at the Social Science Research Unit, Institute of Education, London. She is also Co-Director of the Childhood Research and Policy Centre and Chair of the Planning Team for a new Institute of Education MA on Childhood Studies and Rights. Her current interests include children's rights, citizenship and the UN Convention on the Rights of the Child 1989, special education and inclusion and methods and ethics of research with children. Writing extensively on these themes, she has recently written an article 'Student's rights in British Schools' in *Children, Home and School* by R. Edwards (2002).

Derry Hannam is a Director of the Phoenix Education Trust. Trained as a teacher himself, he taught in comprehensive schools for 21 years before becoming an inspector with Ofsted. He is an adviser to the Council of Europe Education for Democratic Citizenship project and is also involved in teacher training in Eastern and Western Europe.

Jeremy Cunningham is Headteacher at the John Mason School in Abingdon, Oxfordshire. Interested in questions of citizenship and democracy in schools for many years, he has published on issues of participation in school life.

Dr. Liam Gearon is Reader in Education and Director of the Centre for Research in Human Rights at the University of Surrey, Roehampton. His interests range widely, from religion and human rights to literature and censorship in addition to citizenship in education. Amongst other work, he has recently edited *Learning to Teach Citizenship in the Secondary School* (2003) and *Citizenship Through Secondary Religious Education* (2003).

Sally Stenton is a Programme Manager at Changemakers, a charity which encourages young people to address issues of concern to themselves and their community. Focussing on young person-led action, Changemakers works in partnership with schools, youth organisations, local education authorities and other bodies such as education business partnerships. Amongst other projects, Changemakers has recently been heavily involved in the DfES supported Active Citizens in Schools National Pilot.

Carrie Supple is a Programme Manager at the Citizenship Foundation, an organisation founded in 1989 to promote more effective citizenship through education about the law, democracy and society. At the moment her main interest is in Youth Act! Launched this year and based on the internationally successful programme developed by Street Law in the US, Youth Act! is designed to foster young people's political engagement through supporting their initiatives for change.

Sheila Bloom is Director of the Institute for Global Ethics, UK Trust. She has worked in the arts, public relations, and international advertising and marketing, becoming full-time UK Trust Director in 1996. As well as leading seminars, she has co-edited *Ethics and Citizenship: Tools for Moral Decision-Making*, (2002). Focussing on values and citizenship, IGE UK is currently working on three main education projects: an ethics and citizenship teacher resource, the annual Education for Citizenship in England, Northern Ireland, Scotland and Wales conference and the Impetus Awards for Schools and Youth Organisations throughout the UK.

Liz Byrne is Head of Religion and Ethics at the Nobel School, a mixed 11 to 18 Comprehensive School in Stevenage with a particular interest in citizenship and community involvement. In partnership with the University of Hertfordshire, the Nobel School was recently awarded Training School status by the DfES and has received national recognition for raising standards. The school has also twice been recognized as an Investor In People and has won the North Hertfordshire Business Award for Training and Development.

Contributors

Matt Henn and Mark Weinstein are both based at Nottingham Trent University where they teach in the Graduate School of Social and Policy Research with a particular emphasis on research methods. Their own research interests lie in the field of young people and political participation, most recently contributing an article 'Alienation and Youth' to G. Taylor and M. Todd (eds.) *Protest and Democracy* (2003). They are also members of a 'youth and politics' project, focussing on young people's engagement with the political process.

Martin Bratt is a member of the Central Board of the Association of Norweigan Students Abroad (ANSA). Educated at the University of Oslo and the Ecole des Hautes Etudes Commercials in Paris, he has held a number of local and national offices for the Norweigan Young Liberals, including International Officer.

Matthew Green is Liberal Democrat MP for Ludlow. He is also the Liberal Democrat Spokesman on Young People, Education and Skills

Elisabeth Rayment is a researcher at the New Politics Network and is reading History at Merton College, Oxford.

Benjamin Linsley is Communications Officer at the New Politics Network, and Project Manager for the Active Citizenship Project. He is also a school governor and a Labour Councillor in the London Borough of Hackney

Preface

Benjamin Linsley & Elisabeth Rayment

The New Politics Network

Active Citizenship in Education

The introduction of Citizenship in the National Curriculum for 11 to 16 year olds in September 2002 ranks among the boldest changes to secondary education implemented by the present government. Although it received comparatively little attention prior to legislation, slipping almost silently onto the school timetable, the Citizenship Curriculum represented the culmination of many years work and came with suitably high aspirations. A list of practical reasons why its addition to the National Curriculum is a good thing would run into several pages, but the longer-term significance revolves more around its underlying statement of intention than merely the short term 'usefulness' of teaching children good skills. In a country which lacks a written constitution, and whose political culture fears Government prescription like the plague, it is a bold salute to the value of society and community. It is an attempt to provide at least a basic framework of a common value system in a world still at times struggling to face the challenges of the information age and globalisation. Above all else though, it is a recognition of the need to proactively go out and 'make' our future society, and to develop our future citizens, for their sakes as individuals and for all our sakes as members of, and participants in British civic society. Indeed, the Advisory Group on Education for Citizenship concluded in 1998 that:

> "We aim at no less than a change in the political culture of this country both nationally and locally: for people to think of themselves as active citizens, willing, able and equipped to have an influence in public life and with the capacities to weigh evidence before speaking and acting".[1]

One year on, the implementation of this vision has been far from straightforward. The recent Ofsted report into the realisation of citizenship found that there were "significant issues which need to be addressd", more specifically that in over half of the twenty-five schools inspected, "management of the introduction of citizenship has been unsatisfactory"[2]. Though the inspection of Citizenship is at an embryonic stage, and the inspectors themselves add caveats, their findings are a matter of considerable concern. Even Sir Bernard Crick commented: "I may be the father of the movement, but I will strangle the child if it's just a bloody waste of time"[3].

It is clear that many of the questions surrounding citizenship and young people need further discussion. This is particularly the case for active citizenship. Despite being a key part of the Advisory Group's conclusions, the debate so far on 11 to 16 Citizenship has tended to focus on knowledge and understanding. Discussions on the secondary curriculum tend to refer to 'citizenship' and only those on proposals for 16 to 19 to 'active citizenship'. The voluntary nature of Further Education does, of course, imply greater freedom in citizenship education, but it is surely unrealistic to expect young people to suddenly become 'active citizens' on finishing their GCSEs. If we are to see the transformation of political culture envisioned in the Advisory Group's report, the tools of active citizenship must be integral to all education, not a privilege of further study. Key to moving towards this vision and to understanding the full implications of the 11 to 16 Citizenship curriculum, will be explorations of how young people can become active citizens both inside and outside the school community.

Before we begin to discuss active citizenship we must first consider its definition. At first glance it can seem obvious: active citizenship means going out and doing something doesn't it? Yet it must be more than this. Take, for example, the difference between the good and the active citizen. The good citizen is a conformist: an individual who keeps the law, trims the hedge and belongs to Neighbourhood Watch. By contrast, an active citizen is someone empowered to work with others to effect change, to analyse and challenge the status quo. Neither citizen vandalises the local park, both probably vote, yet they are not synonymous. Active citizenship, then, is as much a frame of mind as particular actions. In the desire to participate in society the active citizen possesses a political agency, in the broadest sense, that transcends mere activity. Active citizenship may fit into the third strand of National Curriculum citizenship, 'participation and responsible action', but it cannot be only this. As one eight year old girl remarked to Priscilla Alderson, "it has to be more than picking up litter and not killing whales".

Terms and definitions are rarely perfect and 'active citizenship' is no exception. In an important sense, all citizenship should be active – what, after all, is passive citizenship? Yet as the 1998 Advisory Group recognised, the phrase 'active citizenship' retains a particular resonance. As such it remains the best term to describe the vision of a group of young people engaged with society and empowered to effect change: 'willing, able and equipped'. This project brings together a variety of perspectives: from teachers to politicians, academics to members of the voluntary sector, in order to develop that vision.

With the framework of the Citizenship Order set by Sir Bernard Crick and Tony Breslin, we proceed in Section I to look at the school environment. Independent educationalist John Potter argues the case for a whole school culture of active citizenship; Priscilla Alderson makes the case for developing democratic structures in schools and Derry Hannam explores how school councils can play a part in this. Tying many of these themes together we hear from Jeremy Cunningham, Headteacher at John Mason School in Abingdon, on the day to day experience of delivering a culture of participation and the new Citizenship curriculum.

Section II describes how involvement with the local community is integral to promoting active citizenship. Dr Liam Gearon, looks at why links between schools and their local communities are important, Sally Stenton discusses the potential for young people to be involved through schools. Carrie Supple discusses youth-led initiatives. We then hear about the Impetus Awards from the Director of the Institute of Global Ethics UK Sheila Bloom. Liz Byrne, Citizenship Co-ordinator at the Nobel School, Stevenage, finally describes their experience of connecting a school with the local community.

In the last section, contributors consider wider issues of formal political participation as they affect young people. Dr Matt Henn and Dr Mark Weinstein discuss their recent research into attitudes among young people to politics and political parties, and Matthew Green MP makes the case for enfranchisement at sixteen. For an international comparison we hear from Martin Bratt, on how political parties have engaged young Norwegians. Elisabeth Rayment then considers the place of party youth wings in the broader sphere of youth organisations.

It is clear that citizenship must ultimately encompass every sphere of life. Recognising this we conclude with a piece from Sir Bernard Crick setting citizenship and education within the broader context of initiatives now being developed across government

In this exploration of active citizenship, restrictions of subject and age have set the parameters. The definition of a 'young person' extends at least to 19 and often to 21, but the different questions raised by the debate over citizenship in further education has led us to concentrate on young people aged 11 to 16. Likewise, we have focussed on three particular areas: young people in their immediate school community; the links between young people, schools and the wider community; and wider political culture for young people's participation in formal politics. In doing so, we hope to take further

Preface

the debate on young people as active citizens: to see not just the extraordinary potential of the recent spotlight on citizenship for the transformation of our society, but to suggest ways in which this might be enacted.

Notes:

1.   Final Report of the Advisory Group on Education for Citizenship and the Teaching of Democracy in Schools (Sept.1998)
2.   National Curriculum Citizenship: planning and implementation 2002/3, Office for Standards in Education, June 2003
3.   Quoted in the Times Educational Supplement, 4 July 2003, p12

Why Citizenship At All?

Sir Bernard Crick

Emeritus Professor of Politics, Birkbeck College, University of London, and adviser on citizenship to the DfES 1998-2000

> "The aim of the ancients was the sharing of social power among citizens of the same fatherland: this is what they called liberty. The aim of the moderns is the enjoyment of liberty in private pleasures; and they call liberty the guarantees accorded by institutions to these pleasures."

Benjamin Constant, *'The Liberty of the Ancients Compared with that of the Moderns'* (1820).

Yes, there is ambiguity about what 'citizenship' means, both generally and when thought of as part of an educational curriculum. Sometimes that ambiguity can be helpful. If most of the public did not read 'citizenship' as 'good citizenship' rather than 'active citizenship', there might have been a real political uproar at even a New Labour government setting up an advisory group with very leading terms of reference[1] and then legislating very much along the lines of the report. True, 'active citizenship' was used more strongly and explicitly in the 2000 Citizenship for 16-19 Year Olds in Education and Training report - now not dead and buried, but sitting somewhat anxiously in England's 14-19 curriculum waiting room - but the Citizenship Order of 1999 quite explicitly requires participation both in school and also in the community, and the discussion of issues. The Qualification and Curriculum Authority's (QCA) advisory publication makes clear that both participation and discussion should be about real issues – real to the kids.

Perhaps that ambiguity needs a little theorising. The 1998 report was, of course, a group effort; and if the Chairman did much of the writing, the group was disinclined to let the author of *In Defence of Politics* get away with too much theorising. Some may have been unaware that I was pushing what scholars call civic republicanism: Benjamin Constant's somewhat romantic view of the ancients, and not 'liberalism', as in his somewhat too pessimistic view of the moderns.[2] The Preface to this important gathering, in quoting the overriding aim, shows that the group none-the-less signed up to civic republicanism:

> "We aim at no less than a change in the political culture of this country both nationally and locally: for people to think of themselves as active citizens, willing, able and equipped to have an influence in public life and with the capacities to weigh evidence before speaking and acting".[3]

The term 'citizen' does, however, have two distinct meanings. A citizen can simply be someone who under the laws and practices of a state has both rights and duties, irrespective of the character of that state. But in many states duties can far out-weigh rights, and those rights may not be political at all. Let us take North Korea if only as an extreme example. Most of its inhabitants are citizens, and may properly be called good citizens if they obey the laws and keep their noses clean. But the second sense of being a citizen is what we find in specifically democratic states today when a majority of the inhabitants enjoy the political rights that emerged from a leadership class in the Greek and Roman and early modern city republics. That is to say: free speech, the election of public officers and the right to come together, to change things, big and small; or to prevent undesired changes.

So it seems elementary - except to some nervous head teachers - that there is a difference between being a good citizen and being an active citizen. One can be a good citizen in an autocratic state. One can also be only a good citizen in a democratic state, obeying the law and behaving oneself, minimising offence to others but not working with others to effect or resist change. This good citizen may even vote regularly - if now less than before - may sign a standing-order to support voluntary bodies or pressure groups, but would never attend a meeting. It is this minimalist approach to citizenship that made me, thirty years ago, voice scepticism about an old tradition of Citizenship Education as Civics which stressed the primacy of the rule of law, without encouraging discussion of whether some laws are unjust, work badly and if so how to change them.

> Civic Education is about the civic virtues and decent behaviour that adults wish to see in young people. But it is also more than this. Since Aristotle it has been accepted as an inherently political concept that raises questions about the sort of society we live in, how it came to take its present form, the strengths and weaknesses of current political structures, and how improvements might be made. [..] Active citizens are as political as they are moral; moral sensibility derives in part from political understanding; political apathy spawns moral apathy."
>
> David Hargreaves, The Mosaic of Learning (Demos 1996)

To teach and learn effectively we need to understand and be proud of the theory of free politics and citizenship - however depressing the example of some politicians can sometimes be. Most of us grudgingly or realistically accept that economic theory both describes and legitimizes a price mechanism, but we can forget that there is equally clear political theory that describes and legitimizes democratic societies. Just as economics is concerned with price, that in a world of finite resources everything we want is at the cost of something or someone else, so political theory is concerned with decision-making and persuasion. It is an assertion that, except in times of emergency, societies are best governed politically, not autocratically, that is by public persuasion and publicised compromises among the competing values and interests found in any complex society.

> "The cause of the fallacy into which Plato falls [...] is the wrong premises about unity on which he bases his argument. It is true that unity is to some extent needed, both in a household and in a polis; but total unity is not. There is a point at which a polis by advancing in unity will cease to be a polis. [...] It is as if you were to turn harmony into mere unison or to reduce a theme to a single beat. The truth is that the polis [...] is an aggregate of many members; and education is therefore the means of making it a community and giving it unity."
>
> Aristotle, *The Politics*

Broadly there are two theories of the modern democratic state, mirrored in popular understanding or behaviour. The first dictates that the maintenance of free institutions depends on a high level of popular participation in public affairs, both as a practical necessity and as a moral and civic duty. Whilst the second declares that competitive elections create governments that can modify and uphold a legal order under which individuals can lead their lives with as little interference as possible from the state and minimal public obligations - to obey the laws, pay taxes, do jury service and vote every few years. Historians and political philosophers call the first, 'civic republicanism' and the second, 'the liberal theory of the state'. The liberal theorists of the state tend to see liberty as the direct relationship between the individual and state defined by legal rights and mediated by the market. The civic republican theorists see the guarantors of liberty less in such a direct relationship than in the existence of civil society - a term they have revived and popularised. By this they mean all those semi-autonomous organisations and institutions intermediary and mediating between the individual and the state.

The language of the two recent citizenship reports with their stress on 'active citizenship' was that of a revived civic republicanism, but often 'active and good citizenship' was used so as to recognise the need for a moral basis for the means not just the ends of political activity, and what education should seek to encourage and achieve. But the secondary school teacher should be able to presume that the moral basis for good citizenship is there from primary education to be built upon, and worked into real activities and real discussions of adult issues.

The schools' citizenship report itself stated a radical aim on the assumption that, despite our long parliamentary tradition, there has developed what is now often called 'a democratic deficit' in society as a whole. In a changing society we have been living on the political traditions of the past. The aim was to create a general 'political literacy'. 'Political literacy' was a term invented to mean that someone should have the knowledge, skills and values to be effective in public life. And the report had an implied methodology for teaching and learning: that knowledge of institutions is best gained through discussion of real issues and becoming aware of what institutions are relevant and needed to influence or resolve an issue or problem. It was a deliberate break from how Civics used to be taught, simply as knowledge of structures and legal powers of institutions - easily examinable but deathly boring. Now the stress at every level should be on knowledge as needed, say on a 'need to know basis', when and by confronting real issues.

This has not always been grasped by a few who still think, whether in error or for shelter from uncertainty, of old Civics in a paradigm of 'good citizenship' alone and not of 'good and active'. Some schools and youth organisations, indeed some ministers in some speeches, have taken refuge in 'volunteering' - the Millennium Volunteers and all that! All citizenship must involve volunteering at some stage, but not all volunteering involves citizenship.

Cleaning up a field after a rave or a blitz to clean up a local park or children's playground is admirable, as is giving a party in an old people's home; but it is not active citizenship unless the kids are given: (i) some responsibility and scope for initiative in how they carry out the task; (ii) a knowledge base - how could such despoliation or neglect have been allowed to happen at all; and (iii) a task and a process that enhances their skills of discovery and advocacy, attempting to influence local authorities, local firms, councillors or the police, whatever, whoever is relevant. Volunteering becomes citizenship when the volunteers are well-briefed on the whole context, given responsibility about how to organise their actions, and debriefed afterwards in the classroom or listened to in a formal meeting about whether they think the task could have been done better, or was even worthwhile at all. Volunteers are free citizens acting together; they should never be canon fodder, however worthy the organisation they work for, however time-tested - or ossified - its procedures.[4] In a sentence, citizenship has meant, since the time of the Greeks and the Romans, people *acting together* effectively to achieve a reasonably important common purpose.

To come down to earth: what did we mean by "effective education for citizenship"? The 1998 report was a three-legged stool, each leg dependent on the others, but each constructed in a slightly different way. Firstly, *children learning from the very beginning socially and morally responsible behaviour both in and beyond the classroom, both towards those in authority and towards each other.* This happens in any half-way good primary school; so the base is to be built upon. Secondly, *learning about and participating helpfully in the life and concerns of their school and their local communities* – what American educationalists call 'service learning'.[5] Thirdly, *pupils learning about public life and how to make themselves effective in it through knowledge, skills and specific values* -- what some have called 'political literacy'.[6]

Moral values must surely arise from experience if they are to enter into a person's character so that they come instinctively to influence behaviour. Let me end with an example. Four years ago I was in a primary school in the north of England in an absolute war zone. The majority of the children were from unstable or broken homes, with bad parenting also common place - over sixty percent on free school meals. But the school was an oasis of calm. The head said that it had helped that a father had beaten her up for stopping his daughter swearing, which had shocked that seemingly bad and sad non-community into rallying round and seeing to it that the school was not to be touched in that way again. Well, perhaps the former head of the English inspectorate, Mr Chris Woodhead, was right: good teaching can make up for a poor environment, poverty is no excuse. Certainly an almost heroic small band of teachers had achieved good results against the odds, in literacy and numeracy as well as social skills and values. But I doubt if Mr. Woodhead would have approved of the methods.

A class of six-year-olds was sitting on the floor in circle time when one little girl burst into tears triggering off another. The big magic comfort bear was fetched from the Head's room. They both hugged one side of it. "What's the matter, Mary?" Nothing was secret there. She sobbed out that her dad had been picked up the night before from the flat on a drugs charge resisting arrest. "Was yer Mam with you?" No reply; another little girl piped up "No, she works nights -- on the game." I suspect that in a 'good school' the teacher would have reproved that child, bundled the distressed one out of the room double-quick and got back to the planned lesson on road safety. But she caught that ball and turned it into the lesson.

"Is it good to take drugs?", she asked the class. A unanimous roar of "No" and cries of "'tis wicked", "dead wrong", "them's bad". These already street-wise children had been 'well taught', I thought cynically. But very well taught in fact, for the teacher pressed the loudest shouter, "Why is it wrong, Tracey?" "'Cos it get you into trouble". "The police?" "Aye the police; put me brother inside". "Be all right then if you weren't caught?" "Nay, still be wrong". "Why?" "'Cos it mucks you up".

I thought that was a good reply - she had said it was wrong - a 'value statement', I am sure we all agree - but she could also give two pragmatic reasons: one, the law, and the other personal responsibility. She wasn't just saying "I fink; well it's my opinion, ain't it?" - the post-modernism of the streets. The teacher was demanding reasons, like in French schools, not just 'good' responses. But the teacher still didn't let it rest there. "Just muck you up, Mary?" That was almost a question too far, for fighting tears the little girl said, "Nay, 'ole family". I truly felt that I was in at the birth of a class feeling the beginning of moral responsibility to others.

You can put that word responsibility in a good long list of moral or civic concepts to be learned. My report did that quite reasonably. Responsibility, both moral and political alike, was construed into three parts: care and concern for others; premeditation and calculation about what effect actions are likely to have on those others; and staying with consequences if they are not as intended. It is this third aspect that often falls by the wayside in public life, perhaps the essential difference between PR and policy. Such a 'responsibility-way' of thinking can be learned early, but if it isn't, it can be hard to find later. I have been puzzling about quite what Sir Kevin Tebbit, Permanent Secretary at the Ministry of Defence, meant when he concluded his evidence at the Hutton Inquiry with: "I have felt a deep sense of responsibility, not of culpability but of responsibility." A politically literate person might find it hard to see the difference.

Notes

1. "To provide advice on effective education for citizenship in schools - to include the nature and practices of participation in democracy; the duties, responsibilities and rights of individuals as citizens; and the values to individuals and society of community activity" - *Terms of Reference of the Advisory Group on Citizenship 1998*
2. Even if his pessimism catches what many of us mean by 'the consumer society' - shopping, sport and sex as the most valued human activities
3. *Final Report of the Advisory Group on Citizenship 1998*
4. I will not now set a cat among the pigeons by asking how many famed voluntary bodies encourage participation relevant to policy among their members and employees? Grant-giving bodies seldom consider this small point. Trustees are often not too fond of democracy at home.
5 Alas, we cannot say 'community service' for the Home Office have criminalised that good old term!
6. See my *Essays on Citizenship* (Continuum, 2000) and (editor) *Citizens: Towards a Citizen Culture* (Blackwell and The Political Quarterly, 2001).

Section I

The School Environment

Think Different!
Citizenship Education and the School of the Future

Tony Breslin

Chief Executive, The Citizenship Foundation

Citizenship: towards a new type of 'subject'

The conception of Citizenship offered in each of Sir Bernard Crick's reports[1] and now articulated as the definition of Citizenship that underpins provision both in the National Curriculum and the proposed 16-19 entitlement[2] appears to be straightforward enough. It offers three dimensions: social and moral responsibility, political literacy and community involvement.

The reality is much more complex and, indeed, enriching. For social and moral responsibility read the full breadth of the rights and duties continuum and all that is contested in it. For political literacy read a full range of literacies that, in common parlance at least, go significantly beyond the political: to the social, economic and legal and then beyond. And for community involvement take account of the broader relationship between the school or college and the community it serves. This then is far from the traditional associations of the term and certainly does not constitute what my colleague at the Citizenship Foundation and a key architect of the new curriculum, Don Rowe, refers to - disapprovingly - as 'simply a new civics'.

Moreover, when one considers the recent place of Citizenship in the school curriculum, the challenge of making this new *subject* a success is formidable. Here, I refer to the late, unlamented place of Citizenship as one of six "cross-curricular themes"[3]. While a small number of school's took the opportunities offered by the cross-curricular themes and skills, introduced as part of the initial model of the National Curriculum, to bring coherence and variety to a curriculum framework that otherwise replicated that of a 1950s grammar school, in most they showed barely above the surface. Thus, the crux of Whitty, Rowe and Aggleton's early work on the matter[4] was that to be 'cross-curricular' in a subject-dominated timetable was, as I have argued elsewhere[5], to be, in effect, "everywhere but nowhere". While there were exceptions, school departmental and meeting structures, teachers' professional traditions and subject identities and the absence of a clear place on the timetable and, therefore, in the budget stream conspired to limit the impact of these worthy add-ons: schools it seems were simply not built for cross-curricularity. The result was that Citizenship, Economic and Industrial Understanding and their fellow travellers were, in effect "left to chance". As Shelton and Rowe (1998) observed in the submission that they made to the first Crick committee on behalf of the Citizenship 2000 group, this was simply unacceptable. However one feels about the detail of the new curriculum or about the political motivations and the reports that gave rise to it, Blunkett's and Crick's achievement, as Davies (2004, forthcoming) points out, has been to take Citizenship on from the hit and miss position to one of a Foundation Subject, firmly within the National Curriculum, rather than on its edges.

Just as the term 'citizenship', though, has a baggage, so does the notion of a 'subject'. As one nationally esteemed retired head put it to me in the friendly combat of a seminar a couple of years ago: "you can't teach Citizenship in 45 minute lessons Tony, you'll bore the kids to death". Notwithstanding that she *was* talking about the 'old Civics' and that concerns about boredom have rarely figured high in the minds of curricular planners, there was something in her point: not that Citizenship can't or shouldn't be taught in 45 minute lessons - key aspects of it can be and should be - but that it cannot be taught in 45 minute lessons alone. The risk for Citizenship in its new place as a full member of the National Curriculum is that it takes on too many of the traditions of what has come to be a school subject: that it can only be taught in certain ways by certain people in certain allocations of time and so on. The complexity and depth of Citizenship, post Crick, and as set out above, is simply too rich for this. If Citizenship as a cross-curricular theme was *less than* a subject, as a Foundation Subject, it is critical that it is understood as being *more than one*. As John Potter (2002) points out "citizenship is uniquely challenging in relation to curriculum development because it touches on every aspect of the life and work of the school. It is as much to do with processes as content, relationships as performance". This notion of Citizenship as a new kind of subject, embracing much more than the conventional understanding of what a subject is, has major implications for how it is delivered through the curriculum, how it is taught, by whom and how it is assessed.

Teaching Citizenship: dimensions of delivery

Accepting the multi-faceted nature of citizenship learning is a starting point for grasping the model of the subject that is being advanced here. I want to contend that effective Citizenship Education programmes are likely to combine a variety of delivery channels rather than advocate one in favour of the others. Elsewhere, I have suggested that the framework of the School Citizenship Manifesto can serve to bring these different dimensions of delivery together[6]. Whatever, the best provision is likely to be characterised by a combination of:

- *Discrete provision:* Citizenship 'lessons', identified as such on the timetable and within any broader framework such as the one that PSHE might provide;

- *Cross-curricular support:* Themed and clearly identified work within other subjects of the curriculum which complements that undertaken in the discrete sessions;

- *Events and activities:* Off timetable, and sometimes off site, provision that might include mock elections, court visits, school industry days, community placement programmes and charitable projects;

- *Student participation:* opportunities for students to be involved in the broader life of the school whether this be through membership of a class, year group or school council, through joining an interview panel for new appointments or through representing the school and their peers on some local forum or other.

In such a model the Citizenship lessons[7] provide the anchorage points for the cross-curricular support and the learning that takes place through student participation in the wider life of the school. Where provision is purely cross-curricular, learning is rarely identified by teacher or student as *Citizenship* learning[8]. However, where a clearly branded Citizenship programme is in place then other subjects can meet their own objectives and those of the Citizenship curriculum by supporting it. Studying the suffragettes in History becomes a piece of Citizenship learning when there is a clearly defined Citizenship programme to relate this learning to. Moreover, frequent Citizenship events play a vital role in genuinely distinguishing Citizenship from other subjects and in acknowledging that the lesson alone is insufficient for the delivery of *all* of the learning. Where, the Mathematics or English curriculum might benefit from a special event - a mathematics trail around the town centre or the visit of a journalist - the Citizenship curriculum requires these kind of inputs.

Only in this way can learning about democracy, about the local community, about legal process, about the nature of negotiation and decision-making be consolidated and made real. Thus, as I shall argue in more detail later, effective Citizenship Education has the potential to contribute to the transformation of the nature of the school both *as* a community and *in* the community, impacting on the kind of places schools are and the sort of profession that teaching is in the process. First, though it is important to offer some observations on the context for learning that schools currently offer.

Schools as Institutions: their impact on teachers as innovators

I have written at length elsewhere on the future development of the teaching profession and the impact of schools as institutions on the work of teachers, the learning of students and the ambitions of innovators[9]. The gist of my argument is threefold.

First, it is inappropriate for teachers to pursue a traditional model of professional identity because this involves a process of social distancing and hierarchy that is at odds with both their role as educators - as givers rather than holders of knowledge - and with a society that is increasingly less deferential and, at times, downright sceptical about the claims of altruistic intent that professionals have traditionally made. This decline in deference has had a particular impact on schools. Designed in the nineteenth century for *that* century, the structure of the secondary school in particular has become less and less effective in a world where neither students nor parents are deferential to those 'with an education' or the institutions they work in. As more have gained from the benefits of a universal education, they have become less subservient to it and more demanding of it[10].

Second, the modern secondary school remains modelled on much earlier institutional forms - the factory, the prison, the psychiatric hospital - and that the resultant focus on structure and order has been, at times, at the cost of learning and, certainly, at the cost of *innovation* in learning[11], not least because total institutions of this type both maximise the feeling of change and minimise its impact. Thus, teachers feel - here my evidence is anecdotal but it is the anecdote of every teacher that I know and it squares with my own experience as a teacher - that they are constantly dealing with change and yet curricular structures remain essentially the same as they have been for the better part of the twentieth century.

Third, a consequence of such institutional settings is to institutionalise and isolate those who work in them, notably teachers. In this context, the creativity of teachers is focused increasingly on making schools work as institutions rather than to devising new curriculum structures, approaches to learning and so forth. Ironically, the focus of the current school improvement drive on league table performance and the meeting of quantitatively defined targets, whatever its benefits, strengthens this institutional mindset and as such can inhibit rather than inspire innovation. Concerns around inclusion coupled with a developing critique around the school curriculum and around how well equipped schools are to meet the emergence of a new knowledge of learning have though had a positive counter impact and given rise to a range of pressures for change.

Citizenship and the Rethinking of Teaching: the school as a multi-professional community

Schools have long had a tradition of involving guest speakers and visiting experts in their learning programmes. Traditionally, though, their participation has tended to be fairly ad hoc - often arising from teachers' friendship networks and the like - and limited to certain areas of the curriculum or the life of the school, for instance:

- Careers Education and Guidance programmes - the 'careers talk';

- aspects of vocational and work related learning - preparing for work experience;

- assembly programmes - where often the visitor's contribution is focused on some aspect of values or ethos;

- aspects of PSHE - especially difficult issues that teachers feel uncomfortable or inexpert handling: sex, drugs or alcohol;

- providing support for identified students - from the musically talented to the behaviourally challenged

More recently, though, there is some evidence that these 'outsider inputs' are growing in significance and that, through conduits such as the Connexions framework and the Excellence in Cities initiative, the insiders are becoming established as members of the school's professional community. Thus, it is now common to find:

- school based mentoring and guidance frameworks led by non-teachers;

- 'out of school hours learning' programmes led or supported by non-teachers;

- an increased number of non-teaching support staff such as bursars and classroom assistants;

- lunch time clubs and the like facilitated by members of the local youth service or by community groups.

Thus, non-teachers are moving to the core of the school's staffing structure and working increasingly collaboratively with teachers, often bringing a different adult-student relationship to the classroom or the corridor in the process. One upshot of this development is clear: *schools are increasingly emerging as multi-disciplinary and multi-professional sites*. Here, the Citizenship curriculum is likely to be both a major driver and beneficiary.

As set out above Citizenship is a new kind of subject: more than a subject in the traditional sense. For this reason it needs to be delivered through a range of curriculum spaces - including some that have not traditionally been thought about as 'curricular' at all such as the assembly programme - and through a range of strategies. These spaces and strategies include the traditional ground of the teacher, the 45 minute lesson, and much more: the mock election, the mini-enterprise scheme, the charitable initiative, the court visit, the community project, the human rights day, the school council. Here, the teacher's role is often likely to be as the coordinator or leader of learning rather than as the individual solely responsible for its delivery. Here, the input of a youth worker or local sports personality, a local barrister or social worker, a local councillor or MP, a community leader or local entrepreneur - not as an exotic visitor but as a core player in the programme - is likely to enhance learning and to broaden its reach. The involvement of such individuals becomes key not marginal, normal not exotic, systematic and not ad-hoc, based upon curriculum rationale rather than simply awkward gaps in content.

And because the mode of delivery is necessarily different and broader, a greater range of learners are involved. The student who sometimes struggles or is troublesome in the classroom can excel in the community project or the school council while the solid, if complacent, classroom performer learns that they still have areas to conquer: public speaking, negotiation, working in a non-school environment. The student who struggles to get on with the teacher immediately strikes up a friendship with the youth worker - even if the latter poses a challenge to the school's dress code.

The result is a more inclusive setting and one more likely to encourage greater achievement. The emerging knowledge about individual learning styles and so called 'brain based learning'[12] finds much easier application in the multi-faceted Citizenship Education programme than it is likely to in the established pedagogy of many conventional subjects.

And, if Citizenship as a curriculum benefits from the emergence of the school as a multi-professional community, it also drives this transformation, simply because this type of multi-faceted and multi-professional input is essential to meeting the curriculum's objectives, not least in the community involvement sphere. While inspection guidance on good practice in this area[13] stops short of demanding multi-professional delivery it does advocate the use of a variety of management, teaching and assessment strategies that is far richer than is the case in other 'mainstream' subjects. Perhaps unusually, 'think different' is the call not just from curriculum progressives but also from the inspectorate itself.

Beyond School Improvement: citizenship and the school of the future

A number of authors have argued that we are now reaching the limits of the school improvement agenda as currently conceived[14]. This belief stems from two related concerns.

Firstly, there is the view that there exists a tension at the heart of the broader educational policy agenda between achievement and inclusion. Thus, the more successful schools and teachers bcome with the majority of their students, the more excluded the less successful ones will become. Moreover, it is contended, the gains made in the pursuit of ever more challenging targets are likely to become increasingly marginal. Here, the call is for a better balance between raising achievement and securing inclusion: inclusion does not simply disappear as achievement rises along a straight-line graph. Rather, smaller and smaller gains in achievement are at the cost, within schools and across communities, of creating a rump of excluded youngsters.

Secondly, there is the view that many schools are close to maximising performance given the way that they are currently organised. For a school in such a situation an ever more exacting set of increasingly hard-to-attain targets results not in still higher achievement but in the disappointment of an inevitable plateau in performance and progressive teacher burn-out.

Thus, attention has turned increasingly to a post targets agenda where the focus is less on narrowly defined notions of school *improvement* and more on school *transformation*. The logical analysis behind this is straightforward: if performance is peaking in the current setting, further progress will only be delivered by changing the setting itself. And transformation derives from the introduction of new approaches to curriculum, to learning and to schooling itself. Citizenship Education has something to offer on each of these fronts. That is, and to reiterate, it introduces to the curriculum not simply a new subject but a new *type* of subject which requires:

- a different kind of curricular space and a different approach to curriculum planning;

- a broader perspective on teaching and learning that is likely to involve a new level of collaboration between teachers and other professionals in the teaching process coupled with a greater variety of teaching approaches;

- a reconsideration of how the school functions as a community, notably with regard to the extent to which it welcomes pupil and parental engagement in place of conventional ordered hierarchy;

- a reconsideration of how the school functions in the community, notably with regard to how open it is, especially to local community and business groups and to those who have had a negative experience of traditional schooling.

And such a subject is likely to prosper in a school setting that is:

- family friendly, community focused and child centred;

- based around a curriculum which places the knowledge, values and skills of Citizenship explicitly at the heart of its curriculum;

- multi-occupational and multi-professional in its staffing;

- rich in the range of ways that it engages parents and families;

- inclusive and multi-faceted in its approach to learning, language and the curriculum;

- 'In tune' with the evolving needs of the communities that it serves but not insular in this support;

- accessible to the community during standard school hours, at the weekend and in evenings;

- less of a total 'institution' with softer boundaries and more entry points for a wider range of participants and, therefore, less of a 'school' and more of a 'community learning centre'.

In such a model achievement is not sacrificed for inclusion. Rather, inclusion is seen as the foundation on which greater achievement is built. As the school improvement agenda realises its potential, the time is right to begin to think innovatively about the nature of schooling itself and about the shape of the school of the future. And in any such thinking, Citizenship Education and a consideration of what it means to be a citizenship-rich school - or more simply a citizenship school as Alexander (2001) calls it - must play a key role.

Notes

1. QCA, 1998, FEFC, 2001, Home Office, 2003
2. DfEE, 2000
3. Prince, 2004, forthcoming
4. Whitty, Rowe and Aggleton, 1994
5. Breslin, 2001
6. Ibid
7. And the events and activities if they are sufficiently frequent and clearly identified as Citizenship occasions

Tony Breslin

8.   Whitty, Rowe and Aggleton,1993
9.   Breslin, 2002, 2004 forthcoming
10.   Breslin, 2002
11.   Dalton, I., Fawcett, R. and West-Burnham, J.,2001
12.   Gardner, 1983
13.   OFSTED, 2002
14.   See, for instance, Dalton, Fawcett and West Burnham and his contributors, 2001

References

Alexander, T. (2001) *Citizenship Schools*, Campaign for Learning, London

Breslin, T. (2001) *A Citizenship Manifesto for Every School?* in 'Teaching Citizenship', Vol.1, No.2) Association for Citizenship Teaching, London

Breslin, T. (2002) *Chasing the Wrong Dream? The quest for teacher professionalism and the emergence of the citizenship school* in Johnson, M. and Hallgarten, J., 'From Victims of Change to Agents of Change: the future of the teaching profession', Institute for Public Policy Research, London

Breslin, T and Dufour, B. (2004) *Citizenship and the School of the Future* in

Breslin, T. and Dufour, B. (eds) 'Developing Citizens: effective citizenship education in the secondary school social curriculum', Kogan Page, London

Dalton, I., Fawcett, R. and West-Burnham, J (2001) *Schools for the 21st Century*, Pearson Education / Secondary Heads' Association, Leicester

Davies, I. (2004) *Citizenship and the National Curriculum*, in Breslin, T. and Dufour, B. (eds) 'Developing Citizens: effective citizenship education in the secondary school social curriculum', Kogan Page, London

DfEE (2000) *National Curriculum in Citizenship*, DfES, London.

FEFC (2001) *Citizenship for 16-19 Year Olds in Education and Training*, FEFC, Coventry

Gardner, H. (1983) *Frames of Mind: the theory of multiple intelligences*, Basic Books, New York

Home Office (2003) *The New and The Old: The Interim Report for Consultation of the "Life in the United Kingdom" Advisory Group*, Home Office, London

Prince, L. (2004) *Education for Employability and the Workplace* in Breslin, T. and Dufour, B. (eds) Developing Citizens: effective citizenship education in the secondary school social curriculum, Kogan Page, London

Potter, J. (2002) *Active Citizenship in Schools; a practical guide to developing whole school policy*, Kogan Page, London

QCA (1998) *Education for Citizenship and the Teaching of Democracy in Schools*, OCA, London

Shelton, I. and Rowe, D. (1998) *Citizenship Programmes in Schools and Colleges*, Citizenship 2000, London.

Whitty, G., Rowe, G. and Aggleton P. (1994) *Subjects and Themes in the Secondary School Curriculum in Research Papers in Education*, Pre-publication draft copy, Institute of Education, University of London.

A Whole School Perspective

John Potter

Author of '*Active Citizenship in Schools: A Good Practice Guide to Developing a Whole School Policy*'

A Whole School Approach

Active citizenship must be learnt in a real life context. It is as much about practice as theory. This demands a whole school approach towards something that is both a statutory foundation subject and a requirement that schools promote democratic student participation across and beyond the life of the school.

The 'citizenship triangle' (overleaf) offers a practical and effective way of creating an environment in which citizenship education can flourish. This 'triangle' was developed by the Four Nations (UK) Conference on Citizenship Education and Community Awareness. It brings together:

- the social and political issues that face the school with

- the culture / ethos of the school and

- the ways in which citizenship and community awareness is taught and learnt through the curriculum.

The 'case study' that follows illustrates these points and shows how a whole school strategy is essential if Citizenship Education is to achieve its goals. In our example, Middleton Community School is a secondary comprehensive school, but the same principles apply to Primary and Special Schools.

The citizenship triangle offers a useful framework within which to develop policies, projects and schemes of work for Citizenship Education.

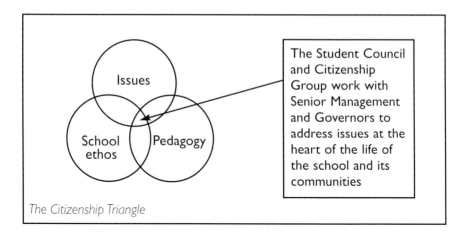

The Student Council and Citizenship Group work with Senior Management and Governors to address issues at the heart of the life of the school and its communities

The Citizenship Triangle

A Case Study

The following case study is assembled from activities and initiatives that are being developed in a number of different schools across the country. An extensive, searchable list of real-life case studies is readily available[1] for those interested in finding our more. However, with few exceptions most schools are in the relatively early stages of developing their Citizenship Education strategy. For that reason the following composite study gives a fuller picture of what a Citizenship programme can look like.

Social and political issues
The Senior Managers and Governors at Middleton Community School have long been aware of the particular social and economic problems facing the communities it serves. Middleton has suffered from long-term unemployment. Many of the more ambitious young families have moved out of the area. There is a large and growing population of old people and most of the teenagers consider the town to be boring. There have been a couple of incidents in which senior citizens were mugged, and the local paper carried articles about 'Teenage Terror'.

The Governors have worked with the Senior Management Team to develop strategies that consciously address:

- mutual understanding between the generations;

- communication within the home - a parents group;

- social enterprise by young people designed to stimulate interesting activities for young people. - The older pupils were responsible for persuading the Council to build a skateboard rink in Middleton Park.

The Senior Management team in consultation with the Governors and School Council have produced a *Citizenship Manifesto*[2] that sets out clearly the way citizenship education is developed at Middleton Community School alongside the entitlements that each child can expect to enjoy in relation to:

- involvement in the School Council[3] and its range of activities;
- whole school projects (by year group);
- subject-based learning.

The culture / ethos of the school

Members of Middleton Community School staff have worked hard over the years to compensate as best they can for the costs of 'communication breakdown' in the area. Sustained efforts have been made to relate to parents and community groups. There is a good relationship with the feeder primary schools, social services and the Connexions Service. A youth worker is linked to the school and works closely with teachers when their time permits.

School Council: From Classroom to Town hall.
Over the past two years the School Council has been restructured to link class Circle Time with elections to the Year Council. Pupils from the School Council regularly report to Governors meetings, and there is a town-wide forum, The Voice of Middleton Students (VoMS). This includes young people from the three secondary schools and the FE College. Recently progress has been made for example over securing cheaper student bus passes.

Every five years there is a general election and the School Council is elected by year groups according to different voting systems. History and humanities lessons give time to issues surrounding the electoral process. They have produced information on the school intranet. Every Year 8 pupil takes part in a debate in the town hall on a topical issue and Year 9 pupils do a project linked with the local Magistrates' court. Public record of this involved is uploaded to the school intranet and forms the subject of assemblies.

Mentoring
There are a number of initiatives to involve pupils in the way the school is run. Last year, following the example of a school in County Durham, the Governors supported a new policy whereby every student at Middleton Community School joined a school-wide mentoring programme.

Mediation
A peer mediation programme has been set up and volunteer pupils selected and trained to tackle disputes between pupils before they become so serious

as to be reported to staff. For over a year the Student Council - with adult professional support - has run a 'Say No to Bullying!' campaign.

Peer Education

There is a paired reading programme between Year 11 and Year 7. Year 8 pupils work with children from feeder primary schools on a Reading Together project.[4] Induction training is provided for all mentors, peer educators and tutors.

Citizenship Day

Each year for the past three years Middleton Community School has held a Citizenship Day. The timetable is suspended. The morning is devoted to sets of workshops on themes proposed by the School Council and the Citizenship Steering Group. Subjects include:

- creating a sustainable environment;

- how fair trade affects Middleton;

- IT projects for parents - tutored by pupils;

- plans for the Middleton Town Festival;

- a Work Fair explaining new employment opportunities opening up in Middleton. In the afternoon the community is invited to Open Day events including sports, drama and music and a presentation of the Fairways Project. The Last hour is an open debate on the future needs of Middleton.

Students write articles on the event and submit them to the Middleton Echo. Local journalists offer students writing and editing training. This coming year Citizenship Day will be broadcast live on local radio. Several students will act as interviewers.

Welcome to Middleton Community School

Students work closely with staff in producing the Citizenship Manifesto a leaflet about the school and its commitment to citizenship education. Students also help run the reception desk in the school entrance and regularly take visitors on guided tours of the school.

Active citizenship in the Middleton

Students are systematically involved in projects that reach out into the wider community.

Critical Success Factors

Middleton Community School has developed and agreed a brief set of critical success factors in the form of a set of simple questions.

- Does our citizenship activity / learning address real issues?

- Does every member of our school community have a voice in the school?

- Do we see all that we do as a chance to learn and a chance to help?

- How can we do even better?

As part of this question the Student Council has agreed with the Citizenship Group to improve communications. The Fairways Project is part of this initiative.

Current themes
'Everyone is a local and global citizen'

Year 7 Learning Matters	Peer learning projects linked with primary school
Year 8 Earth Matters	Building a sustainable school and community environment
Year 9 Community Matters	Cross generation projects with older people and young children
Year 10 Communication Matters	Investigation, research, reporting and policy across and beyond the school

Year 11 & 12 Themes are selected by students on biannual basis. That is, Year 11 selects an issue to pursue in depth and breadth over the following two years.

Pedagogy

Themes by Year Group

There are many ways of tackling citizenship and community awareness. The challenge is to make it an entitlement within the taught curriculum.

Middleton Community School in association with its primary feeder schools and the local Special School has approached the question by identifying project themes that can be developed across year groups. These themes remain relatively stable from year to year and can be associated with projects in school and the town. As far as possible these themes respond to the social issues formally identified as facing the school and its communities.

Each theme is treated from both the local and the global perspective under the banner "Everyone is a local and global citizen". Staff and pupils are clear that the themes can be adjusted and developed in the light of their shared experience. Members of staff are clear that it is the choice of Middleton School to work in this way and that there is no rigid requirement from government to do so. They welcome the flexibility in the curriculum requirements for citizenship education. Members Steering Group who applied for the BT Citizenship Award (Project) realise that because they had a strong structure for Citizenship Education across the school, they were well placed to make the most of the opportunity that the BT Award gave them.

Teaching and Learning

Citizenship and community awareness education offers teachers opportunities to develop a range of experiential approaches to learning, which fosters understanding and skills in the context of community involvement. The principles of this approach to pedagogy are referred to in the United States as 'service learning'. Very simply put: young people are given structured opportunities to acquire knowledge, understanding and disposition through activities that benefit other people. For many teachers this approach revisits pedagogies taught in the 70s and early 80s.

The Get Global[5] programme develops this strategy in its teaching materials. The Citizenship Group at Middleton Community School decided to use these materials as the basis of their curriculum development as they supported the school's Citizenship motto - 'Everyone is a local and global citizen'

Ambition and caution

Our fictitious institution, Middleton Community School, had an Ofsted inspection in the autumn of 2002. They were praised for their ambitious and strategic approach to Citizenship Education. The inspectors liked the way school policies underpinned Citizenship Education across and beyond the curriculum. They were impressed with the variety and quality of evidence collected by pupils in relation, for example, to the Fairways project. They accepted that not all the ambitious strategies that Middleton Community School staff had developed for Citizenship Education were in place yet. "It is, after all, an emerging subject" they said encouragingly. They particularly liked the 'Citizenship Day' and all that contributed to it.

They had one criticism. Citizenship Education in some subject areas was not always clear or understood to be Citizenship Education. For example, the history teacher – an able and enthusiastic person – spent time teaching about how the suffragettes won the vote for women (History). He did not engage the pupils in reflecting on what they felt about voting now, and how they and others might improve participation (Citizenship.) The same point applies, for example, to communication. It is true that all communication can contribute towards effective social relations and civic engagement. However, good communication in itself is NOT citizenship. It becomes citizenship when it contributes consciously to the quality of public life.

Conclusion

Citizenship Education offers schools an opportunity to do more than introduce a new and potentially stimulating subject into the whole and taught curriculum. It further opens up opportunities for the school to develop fresh and dynamic approaches to teaching and learning as part of their strategies for improvement. It can also be the occasion for a new deal with pupils, parents and the many stakeholders from the local community. Citizenship Education is more than a subject; it is a way of learning and the means to developing stronger and more vibrant communities.

Notes:

1.   http://www.csvcommunitypartners.org.uk
2.   The Manifesto is an idea first mooted by Tony Breslin, Chief Executive of the Citizenship Foundation. For further information go to http:// www.citizenshipfoundation.org.uk
3.   For further information, go to http://www.schoolcouncils.org
4.   Reading Together is a paired reading initiative promoted by CSV. Training and materials are available. See Section V. Preparing, Developing and Showcasing your projects – Helpful Organisations
5.   Further details of this excellent programme are available on the websites of the supporting organisations. See, for example www.actionaid.org/schools and /youth

Democracy in Schools
Myths, Mirages and Making it Happen

Professor Priscilla Alderson

Professor of Childhood Studies, Social Science Research Unit,
Institute of Education, University of London

D emocracy in schools tends to be seen as an abstract topic to be taught, rather than a reality to be lived. This article reviews some of the myths used to explain and justify why schools have to be undemocratic, and why democracy can only be taught through undemocratic methods. Mirages or misperceptions among educationalists that emerge from these myths are then considered, showing the contradictions and chasms between the aims, methods and outcomes in many schools. The final section reports on how students and teachers are working together to create democratic schools.

Myths about democracy in schools: how true are they?

Democracy is a great but unrealistic idea.

Partly true. A glance around the world's democracies shows that they cannot wholly resolve conflicts of interests and values among all their citizens, or ensure that everyone's voice is heard, let alone acted upon fairly. However, there is a general view that other systems are far worse than democracy, and that it is better to attempt to organise societies as democratically as possible than to resort to other systems. If this view applies to international, national and local communities, then why should it not apply also to schools?

Democracy can only exist in communities of mature adults citizens

False. To be a citizen is an automatic right, and does not have to be earned by being 'mature'. If maturity means being rational, informed, wise, tolerant and responsible, then many adults often behave immaturely, and are irrational, selfish and foolish. They do not then necessarily forfeit any of their democratic rights. Democracy relies on having a responsible majority, but it also has to be strong enough to include all kinds of people. Many children are altruistic and rational. There is no direct correlation between maturity and adulthood.

The main activity in schools is to develop and socialise children
Schools turn young 'barbarians' into 'civilised men' (Peters 1965:43)

False. Young children tend to start school with their life-long knowledge, practical moral relationships, and understanding of social obligations already well established. (Damon, Dunn, Gardner, Mayall, Miller) When schools infantilise their students of all ages ('infant' meaning without speech and, in practice, not heard) then students are likely to regress and rebel or retreat into apathy. True, schools are mainly places for expanding knowledge and skills, changing and learning, selecting and forgetting, but these activities are not unique to schools or to childhood, we do them throughout life. We change qualitatively, but there is not an essential change from zero, the barbarian-child, up to an endpoint of the socialised-adult, in the way tadpoles turn into frogs. Young school children are already social, moral persons, tending to behave like the adults closest to them.

Adults must maintain strict control in schools and therefore autocratic hierarchies are the only option.

False. Yes, adults have duties of care, and ought to ensure that schools are safe and orderly, although many schools are not. Adults can only really promote order and harmony by working with the students, not in opposition to them. And working with others involves respectful listening and negotiation on both sides. Nation states powerfully demonstrate how democracy is linked to social order, and autocracy to injustice and discord. Those who assert the myth that schools must be undemocratic therefore have to answer the question: Why should schools be an exception to the known links between democracy and orderly communities versus non-democracy and disorder? (There are orderly hierarchies, such as religious communities, but people tend to choose to enter and to stay in them, through a form of democratic consent. Schooling is compulsory.)

Democracy concerns impersonal political systems

Partly true, the systems are vital. But the principals of democracy are also expressed or violated through social and personal relationships. These exist along a spectrum from respect and free choice at one end, to coercion and violence at the other. We live between these extremes, sometimes appropriately stressing one end or the other. The balance becomes more complicated when we move beyond individual and into group relationships, as in schools. Teachers, like governments, often deny individuals' rights, claiming that this benefits the majority. Democratic principles offer the means of analysing and negotiating how to balance the great and partly conflicting values of equality, liberty and solidarity, through general systems and also personal relationships.

Democracy in schools should mainly involve teaching political literacy

False. This myth assumes that teaching about democracy mainly involves conveying sets of ideas and facts, often abstruse and remote ones, and usually about how adults organise democratic processes. It presents democracy as a dull theory instead of as an intensely important, interesting and emotive living reality, such as disputes on sharing control and resources that affect everyone.

Democracy in schools 'for citizenship' mainly concerns preparing young people for future adult citizenship.

False. This myth treats school students as human-becomings, and less than fully human-beings. It is illogical to suppose that children can learn and understand concepts of justice, freedom of the press, or due process of law, and yet not notice or mind that these rights are denied to them at school. For example, when they are treated unfairly, their speaking and writing are regularly censored, or they have no right to explain or appeal if, for example, they are suspended. When citizenship and rights are seen as adult privileges, it follows that these are denied to children. If democracy in schools is set in the future away from the present, democracy dwindles into empty rhetoric. Daily practices deny and contradict the precepts that are taught. Students become bored, cynical or angry about the ensuing confusion and hypocrisy. Teachers, often against their own will, preach 'do as I say, not as I do'.

Moving past the mirages and misperceptions

All the above myths about education 'for adult citizenship' and not 'of and with young citizens' support undemocratic schools, which counteract a lot of education about democracy. Educationalists who believe these myths fail to see how unjust and unpleasant so much schooling is. They blame and punish young people if they rebel against conditions that adults would not tolerate. They see mirages of schools as necessarily 'disciplined', or as pleasant productive work places – some schools succeed in being so, but many do not. Here are just a few examples of real life in many schools, beyond the mirages.

Just suppose, as an adult, that you arrive at work and wait outside locked doors in the rain. You queue until you and your hundreds of colleagues are all suddenly allowed in together, struggling through crowded corridors. Up to a quarter of your day is taken up with queuing and marching, often in enforced silence (Griffith 1998). You have no space of your own but work in different parts of a large campus with regular crowded mass treks to the next workspace. You have nowhere to leave your coat and belongings and must carry them everywhere with you. You have a few short break times, but may be 'kept in' as a punishment, with no right of appeal. If you try to appeal, you will only get further punishment. The very unsavoury toilets are locked for most of the day, and over-crowded when you are 'allowed' in. You cannot have anything to drink all day; water fountains are turned off, 'in case you have water fights'. There are petty rules about uniform, jewellery and any hints of personal expression. These in turn stop freedom of speech because if you ask for a forum, such as a council, to review any rules democratically you are told, 'No, because you will only want to talk about uniform and you are not allowed to.' With breakfast club and after-work club you spend about 50 hours a week at work. When you arrive home your partner says, 'Your boss has just phoned to tell me that you have broken that agreement I signed with her. You were late back from lunch and she says I must stop you watching television for a week.' You reply, 'But I was helping a friend whose mobile was stolen.' 'Tough,' says your partner, 'I don't want any more lame excuses. Now get on with that work that has to be ready for tomorrow.' And so on. (From Alderson 2003, and partly drawn from our research on students' views about their rights in schools Alderson and Arnold 1999.)

Before we can have education for democracy in democratic schools we have to correct the misperceptions based on myths that children and young people are so very different from adults. And also that somehow they benefit from, or do not realise, or do not mind, being treated so disrespectfully. We have to see the contradictions and chasms in many schools, between their aims to help their students to be mature responsible citizens, their methods of denying students responsibility and respect, and the outcomes in many schools of high levels of unqualified, disaffected school leavers, with people aged under 35 years being the least likely ones to vote.

Creating democratic schools

It doesn't have to be like this, despite the strong economic and political pressures that force many British schools away from being democratic. A review of the history of schools shows many exciting examples of democracy across the decades although, depressingly, most existed quite briefly and depended on exceptionally inspired teachers. Yet still, around the world, students and teachers are working together to dispel myths and mirages and to create democratic schools. From countless examples, here are just three that illustrate the huge range of struggles towards democracy: one is international, one from Rajasthan, India, and one from London.

International support for democratic schools

The United Nations Convention on the Rights of the Child (UN 1989) promotes 'participation rights'. These include children's rights:

- to respect for their worth and dignity;

- to express their views freely in all matters that affect them, and to have their views taken seriously;

- to develop their skills and talents fully;

- to freedom of information, and of peaceful association and assembly;

- to freedom of thought, conscience and religion;

- to learn to live in peace, tolerance, equality and friendship;

- to privacy, respect and fair discipline;

- to freedom from discrimination and exclusion.

Like all rights, children's rights are qualified and not absolute. The Convention respects children's welfare and safety, and their need - though this cannot be an enforceable right - for supportive parents and a loving family. Far from undermining families and schools, or being selfishly individualistic, the Convention sees children's rights as inalienable to all members of the human family, promoting social progress and better standards of life in larger freedoms, and laying foundations for peace and justice in the world.

The Convention is a tool for change. All governments have ratified the Convention except the USA and Somalia, which has no government. They have to report regularly to the UN on their progress in implementing the Convention in law, policy and practice. The UN Committee on the Rights of the Child (UN 1995, 2003) has criticised the British government for not yet basing teacher education on the Convention, or publicising the Convention widely to adults and children alike, or insisting that students may speak and have a fair hearing if there are proceedings to suspend them from school. The UN Special Rapporteur on Rights to Education has also eloquently criticised Britain's undemocratic education systems (UN 1999, Woodward 2003).

Yet there has been progress. Since 2001, the government has told all its departments to consult children and young people about services for them, including schools. There is a danger that these will be token, selective, and potentially misleading consultations. Much work and training are required to ensure that the consultations are fair, respectful, use sound methods, and are taken seriously in efforts to improve the services. But this is a start.

The Children's Parliament in Rajasthan

The next example shows how democracy can be understood and promoted by young people with little education. Through the 1980s, village night schools opened for working children. The curriculum connects closely with the children's daily life and needs; the teachers are graduates of their own village school. In 1993, the Children's Parliament opened, in order that the children could really influence school policies, besides learning about democracy, the vote, how to stand up for their rights, and about the politics of poverty. The 2,500 children aged 6-14 years elect their 17 MPs aged 11-14 years. The MPs inspect the schools, listen to the students, and may sack lazy teachers. The Parliament helps villages to improve other amenities, such as water supplies. It holds children's festivals, publishes a magazine, and has a consciousness-raising touring puppet show about rights. Far from children being 'socialised' by adults, they are teaching and helping adults, even in this very patriarchal and caste-conscious society. (Srinivasan 1999)

Siobhan in London

The great democratic principles can only truly be respected when put into practice in countless small details. This final example shows one facet of democracy, the equal inclusion of disabled people, and shows how changes can be achieved through the individual efforts of disadvantaged people. Siobhan and her mother fought 'epic battles' for her right to attend her local primary school where she was happy. Siobhan described her move to secondary school when she was 11 years old. (Alderson and Goodey 1998: 142-4).

> "Well that was hard work because there weren't no lifts, and for the first year I was there, lots of teachers had to come to me. First, I had no lessons, I was sitting in reception…some teachers came down to me, some didn't. [It was] kind of horrible, 'cos, see I wasn't mixing with friends…'cos they was all going to their lessons, so it kind of built a barrier a bit. In the end they were rescheduling the lessons, near the end of that year. When the lift was completed it was much better."

Later, more disabled students joined the school and Siobhan felt the teachers came to accept her. Instead of talking down to her, now "they talk to me more personal, suiting my age". Siobhan's mother agreed. Siobhan, and thousands of young people like her, are not only facing the world, they are changing it.

Conclusion

For centuries, leading educationalists have advocated learning by doing, instead of by listening passively to confusing dry abstractions. Even very young and unschooled children can understand complicated aspects of democracy, rights, justice and respect, through their activities and achievements.

Democracy is practical and pervades all relationships. We cannot avoid either 'doing' democracy or else being actively undemocratic; there is no middle way. Undemocratic schools powerfully teach, by example, lessons of intolerance, mistrust, disrespect, repression and fear of change. If they preach democracy, they teach duplicity. Students who try to improve matters learn to fail and to feel powerless and hopeless, a disastrous prelude to adulthood and to the future of democracy. Schools that work to promote democratic approaches demonstrate and encourage the personal strengths of active citizens: listening tolerance and cooperation, respect and equality, trust and hope, being open and adventurous. Such schools gain from the fresh ideas and efforts of many of the students and staff, and not only of the few 'top' people. When students are active citizens in the school community, as the Indian children and Siobhan showed, they learn as much if not more from the extra activities as from the basic curriculum. And, in the words of the UN Convention they lay the foundations for peace and justice in the world.

References

Alderson P 2003 *Institutional rights and rites: a century of childhood*. London: Institute of Education.

Alderson P, Goodey C 1998 *Enabling education: experiences in special and ordinary schools.* London: Tufnell Press.

Alderson P, Arnold S 1999 *Civil rights in schools: ESRC Children 5-16 Programme Briefing no 1*. Swindon: ESRC.

Damon W 1990 *The moral child.* New York: Free Press

Dunn J 1988 *The beginnings of social understanding.* Oxford: Blackwell.

Gardner H 1993 *The unschooled mind.* London: Fontana.

Griffith R 1998 *Educational citizenship and independent learning.* London: Jessica Kingsley.

Kagan J 1986 *The emergence of morality in young children*. Chicago IL: University of Chicago Press.

Mayall B 2002 *Towards a sociology for childhood.* Buckingham: Open University Press

Miller J 1996 *Never too young: how young children can take responsibility and make decisions.* London: NEYN/ Save the Children.

Peters R 1965 *Education as initiation*. Inaugural lecture. London: Harrap for Institute of Education.

QCA – Qualifications and Curriculum Authority 1998 *Education for citizenship and the teaching of democracy in schools* (Crick Report). London: QCA.

Srinivasan S 1999 *Personal communication*, In John M 2003 *Children's rights and power*. London: Jessica Kingsley, 231-9.

UN 1989 United Nations Convention on the Rights of the Child. Geneva: UN.

UN 1995 United Nations Committee on the Rights of the Child. Consideration of reports submitted by State Parties under Article 44 of the Convention. Concluding observations: UK and Northern Ireland. Geneva: UN

UN 1999 Report of the mission on the UK by the Special Rapporteur on the Right to Education. Geneva: UN.

UN 2003 United Nations Committee on the Rights of the Child. Consideration of reports submitted by State Parties under Article 44 of the Convention. Concluding observations: UK and Northern Ireland. Geneva: UN

Woodward W 2003 Interview with Katarina Tomasevski, UN Special Rapporteur on the Right to Education. The Guardian, 14 July.

Student Councils
Education for Democracy in English Secondary Schools

Derry Hannam

Project Director, The Phoenix Education Trust

We are now one year into the implementation of the Citizenship Order in English secondary schools. Although the Order does not statutorily require schools to facilitate the creation of school student councils it nonetheless 'encourages' them to do so and this 'encouragement' is reinforced in Ofsted's 'Inspecting Citizenship 11-16.'

Studies through the 1990's that attempted to gauge the proportion of secondary schools in England having student councils (Fogelman 1991, Ashworth 1995, Alderson 1999, Baginsky and Hannam 1999) found the figure to be around 50%, with the number of councils regarded as being 'effective' by the student body to be around 20%.

It would appear from the Citizenship Education Longitudinal Study: First Cross Sectional Survey 2001-2002 that the 'encouragement' or 'spur' of the Citizenship Order and the Ofsted Inspection guidelines has certainly had an effect on the number of secondary head teachers/school leaders claiming to have student councils in their schools. The survey came up with the slightly astonishing figure of 94% in a randomly selected sample of 200 schools, though this is tempered by the fact that only 64 per cent of students felt that they had any opportunity to be involved in running their school through a student council, and only a third indicated that they had been involved in electing student council members. In fact, the numbers indicating that they had had any degree of participation in proceedings in the last year are 9% for Year 8 and 11% for Year 10 - the survey does not make clear to what level this participation refers, i.e. whether it be class discussion or representative year or school council meeting.

The figure of 94% involves a degree of wishful thinking and future-gazing by some head teachers. A guesstimate would be that the 94% covers the widest possible spectrum from "utterly tokenistic and constrained and regarded with sceptical and deserved indifference by most students", through "early stages of planning – not yet had first meeting", through "launched but struggling to fly", to "well established and seen to be effective by most students", with the proportion at the latter end still at about 20-25% maximum.

This somewhat gloomy view of the current state of student councils in secondary schools is borne out by Ofsted's National Curriculum Citizenship: planning and implementation 2002/03. Although it involved only a small sample of 25 schools, these were not randomly chosen. They had either been recently inspected and reported to be making significant preparations for the implementation of the Citizenship Order or had been recommended by LEA's as being worth a visit. Most, as one might expect given the selection process, had student councils. As the report states, councils:

> "…have the potential to involve all pupils, who can discuss council matters in their tutor groups and elect and make accountable their representatives."

Unfortunately such practice was not the norm even in this selected sample.

> "Some of the school councils fail to involve all pupils through such representation. Some have very limited ambition, with agendas being principally concerned with food and toilets. In a minority of the schools, school council members are appointed by staff rather than elected. In these cases, little or nothing is contributed to National Curriculum citizenship for most pupils."

One can be fairly sure that such councils are not perceived to be 'effective' by most students in those schools! There was some good practice in some of the 25 schools but only one is referred to as 'exemplary'.

So what makes for an 'effective' students' council and why is it so hard to achieve?

The literature is not vast but there are common threads to be found. (Davies 1998, Clay, Gold and Hannam 2001, Hannam 2001, Inman and Burke 2002, Taylor and Johnson 2002, Trafford 2003. It is encouraging that two of these works were published by professional associations, one by the Association of Teachers and Lecturers and another by the Secondary Heads Association, and that a third was funded by the DfES.) They are driven by both principle and pragmatism.

The first absolutely clear point is that a council which is felt by students to offer serious and effective opportunities for participation in school decision making cannot be an add-on extra to a fundamentally authoritarian and coercive institution. It must spring from a deep belief in the right of young people to have a voice. The literature indicates that this belief must be held by the school leadership, the head teacher in particular, and at least a significant minority of the teaching staff. When I conducted a pilot study for CSV/DfES in 2001 (Hannam, 2001) to explore associations between student participation, attendance, exclusion and achievement I found this commitment to the students' voice as of right in all of the 12 selected 'more than usually participative' secondary schools. Some of the schools actually referred to the student council as the principal means for implementing Article 12 of the UN Convention on the Rights of the Child in the school prospectus. This commitment to students' rights shines from the pages of Bernard Trafford's excellent little book 'School Councils, School Democracy, School Improvement.' It is the mainspring of his success with democratic innovation at the independent Wolverhampton Grammar School. (Trafford 2003).

A close second to a commitment to the right of students' to a voice comes the recognition that a democratic participative ethos is associated with enhanced learning, and that some important learning can only take place through the experience of participation in the democratic decision making. The most obvious, and supported by large-scale research, is an understanding of and commitment to democracy itself. Both recent IEA studies, Citizenship and Education in Twenty-eight Countries (Torney-Purta et al 2001) and Civic Knowledge and Engagement in Upper Secondary Students in Sixteen Countries (Torney-Purta et al 2002) conclude that:

> "Schools that model democratic values by…inviting students to take part in shaping school life are most effective in promoting civic knowledge and engagement…and they are more likely to expect to vote as adults than other students."

The authors conclude with the "sting in the tail" that "…this approach is by no means the norm in most countries." The component IEA English Report (Kerr et al, 2002) endorses these findings for 14 year-olds in English secondary schools and agrees that a democratic approach "is by no means the norm" here either.

Of course the improvements that can accrue to learning do not stop at learning experientially about democracy. The democratic participative approach also appears to provide the key to deep learning about associated issues such as human rights, justice and morality. There is also evidence that the democratic participative ethos is associated with enhanced learning across the whole curriculum, especially when the participation includes decision making about what is to be learned, and how, when and with whom it is to be learned. (Hannam 2001, Trafford 2003).

Schools with effective student councils also seem to understand that many other contributions to school improvement follow from effective listening to the student voice and open-hearted sharing in decision making. There is hardly any problem affecting the day-to-day running of a school on which the students do not have a unique and valuable 'take'. These schools take issues of concern to management to the students' council and reciprocally listen carefully and positively engage when students bring their issues to management.

Schools with effective students' councils do not attempt to restrict and constrain what can be discussed though they may well negotiate sensible guidelines. Some would argue that it is necessary to set clear boundaries for what may be discussed, but I stand by the view expressed in the 'Toolkit' that I co-authored for the DfES/School Councils UK (Clay, Gold and Hannam 2001) which is supported by Bernard Trafford (Trafford 2003).

> "Most effective councils do not exclude anything from being discussed, apart from matters of personal confidentiality. The power of councils to make decisions and take action are likely to expand as students become more confident…If rigid limits are imposed on councils at the outset, students are unlikely to develop any enthusiasm for them."

Other criteria for effectiveness indicated by the literature include: –

- high profile support for the students' council from school leadership drawing in the support of teachers, non-teaching staff, parents and governors

- conspicuous reference to the importance of student councils in key school documentation including prospectus and development plan

- getting the structure right so that effective meetings are possible

- the opportunity for meetings to be as frequent and of sufficient length as the business requires

- provision of appropriate accommodation for meetings and access to computing/reprographic facilities - in some Scandinavian Upper Secondary schools that I have visited the students council has its own office with telephone, computer and photocopier

- opportunities for effective meetings to take place in every constituent class and tutor group

- excellent communication and feed-back to and from representative council meetings
- skill development activities for student councillors and teachers who work with them

- regular communication with governors through the presence of elected students as 'associate members' of the governing body. - now formally set out as an option for governing bodies in the new regulations that came into operation for State Community Schools from September 2003

- a budget

- the possibility for at least some meetings to be in 'curriculum time.'

- thoughtful integration of the student council activities and experience into the overall citizenship curriculum

It is encouraging that the DfES has recently published a draft document entitled Working Together: Giving Children and Young People a Say (DfES 2003), which will in time become the official guidance to schools for the implementation of section 176 of the 2002 Education Act. This requires LEA's, governing bodies and schools "…to consider the views of children and young people and involve them when making decisions."

This is a positive step towards the statutory rights to participation in school decision making awarded to secondary students in many other European countries such as all the Scandinavian nations, the Netherlands, Spain and Austria.[1] School students in the four nations of the UK are almost alone in Europe in not having a school students' organisation and thus miss out on many European activities and opportunities to meet and exchange ideas with young people from other Council of Europe member states. However a group of enthusiasts have formed the ESSA (English School Students Association) network which, with the support of the Phoenix Education Trust is actively working towards creating such an organisation.

England is not alone in finding it hard to make student councils work effectively in all secondary schools but it must be said that it is not in the vanguard, and that it has much to learn from the countries such as Norway and Finland that are. Traditional attitudes and anxieties of the teaching profession and in particular expectations of the 'strong head teacher', expectations of some parents and the media, the incorrect association of rigid authority with high academic standards, inappropriate forms of accountability such as league tables that take no regard of social circumstances or the achievements of less academic students, a failure to understand the nature of effective learning, and sheer in-built cultural deficit models of childhood that problematise, marginalise and even criminalise the very existence of young people all play their part and must be tackled.

New developments at the National College for School Leadership give one cause for optimism. Their advocacy of the notion of dispersed leadership which takes in the students as potential leaders in schools is an exciting development. Schools that truly believe in the potential of their students are what we need, with head teachers willing to take risks to allow this potential to develop.

Notes:

1.   These are set out in the Country Guide produced by OBESSU (The Organising Bureau of European School Student Unions) which can be obtained by e-mailing their office in Brussels at obessu@obessu.org or from their website www.obessu.org, and in the shortly to be published All European Study of Student Participation Policies compiled for the Council of Europe by Karlheinz Duer of the State Centre for Political Education in Baden-Wurtemburg, Germany.

Active Citizenship in Practice

Jeremy Cunningham

Headteacher at John Mason School, Abingdon
In conversation with Elisabeth Rayment

John Mason School in Abingdon, Oxfordshire, is one school that has aimed to bring ideas of active citizenship into the culture of the whole school. Headteacher Jeremy Cunningham talked to Elisabeth Rayment.

Lying seven miles south of Oxford, John Mason School is a mixed 11 to 18 community school with 1100 students. Although the number of students with English as a second language is small and those qualifying for free school meals below the national average, its catchment nevertheless draws in students from a wide range of socio-economic backgrounds: "from people who are really struggling, to people who are very well-off". Jeremy Cunningham has been the Headteacher since 1994.

The active involvement of students has been integral to the school for many years, as the third strand of its motto, 'High Standards, Happy School, Honourable Service' bears out. Included in 1994 after staff spent a day away reflecting on the school, highlighting 'Honourable Service' was a response to the feeling "that education was being marketed as an individual right and not as anything to do with a duty for the future". The reworking of the school motto also coincided with the introduction of 'Community Days': opportunities during the summer term for students to explore citizenship issues off-timetable. One of the most successful of these projects has been a day conference entitled 'City Action', where Year 10 visited community projects in the more culturally diverse area of East Oxford. This involved not only visiting projects but also gave students the opportunity to question local politicians about the issues raised in a local area that many students had never visited before.

At John Mason School 'Honourable Service' and participation are not,

45

however, limited to these rare days off-timetable. For some time it has been the belief of the senior management team that the participation of all students through increasing democratisation brings real benefits to the school community. As Jeremy Cunningham comments, "you increase the happiness of the school by having good leadership and responsibility among the students, where they feel it is their school". Though he is unable to say whether or not this increased responsibility raises academic standards, it seems clear to him that this sense of ownership "tends to produce good educational standards, if you think of standards in the round, not merely academic ones".

A key part of this vision of participation has been the work of the Student Council. When he arrived at John Mason, Jeremy Cunningham found Year meetings and a tradition of "students giving their views" but without clear organisation; the developments from there have been gradual, a partnership between staff and students "pushed by some good leadership among the Chairs of the Council". The success of the Student Council lies in its combination of effective representation of the student body, connections with the staff and the power to make real changes to the school. In terms of representation, each form group has two representatives on their Year Council, from which a Chair and Secretary are elected to sit on the main body. The Chair of this central Council has a permanent seat on the Parent and Teachers Association as well as the governing body, and meets with the Headteacher monthly for feedback. The principle of involvement has also led representatives from the Student Council to become involved in the interview process for new staff.

This sense of ownership also applies to the fabric of the school. In recent years one of the Student Council's main campaigns has been for the replacement of the old cycle sheds. The student body initiated the fundraising, holding talent shows, non-uniform days, gigs and discos, raising over £3000. With this money and support from both the PTA and governors the Council then successfully petitioned the Department of Trade and Industry for the remaining £23,000. The school has also been unafraid in using more direct initiatives. Recently, each Year Council was given £200 to spend at the end of the year, with money removed for labour and parts when lockers were vandalised. Giving students an opportunity to see how their actions can affect the school environment, the project resulted in a dramatic decrease in locker damage; a similar scheme is now underway for litter.

This encouragement of active participation in the school goes beyond the Student Council. As Jeremy Cunningham admits, the representatives on the central Council tend to be pupils with developed written or interpersonal skills, and there is a need "to ensure that verbally powerful students or those from other social groups are elected". But other schemes do ensure that participation is not limited to the articulate minority. Students have the opportunity to act as guides for open evenings or work on reception, as "seeing the school at work is at the heart of participation". The experience of representing the school to others is also reflected in a programme that gives Year 8 the responsibility of helping the new Year 7 to settle in. Outside of lesson-time, a Bus Safety Committee gives the older students the responsibility to ensure journeys to school are safe. Members of the committee carrying cards that allow them to report any problems, from arguments between students to unsafe driving, to the bus coordinator. In sport, the school is divided into houses and each class has a leader for school competitions, but older students also have the opportunity to participate through the Sports Leadership scheme. Under this project, "a particular success", the Year 10s are equipped to train primary school pupils, giving them the chance to develop leadership skills as well as representing their school to others. Many Year 10 students have also been enthusiastic about the opportunity to become a reading or writing 'buddy', helping Year 7s with literacy difficulties. In the future, Jeremy Cunningham hopes to extend this system of peer support into other areas. Like most secondary schools he admits that John Mason sees "a degree of conflict between students"; improving these relationships provides particular opportunities for peer mentoring

Of course, the development of student participation has not always been straightforward. At times the Student Council has experienced problems in communicating the details of meetings and keeping minutes, for example. The involvement of the Student Council in a Youth Forum organised by the District Council has also brought mixed results. These forums only involve a small minority of pupils, and although good for increasing political literacy they have, in Jeremy Cunningham's view been ineffective in "actually seeing real change in the community and communicating back to schools". "If they set up a skate park", he comments, "they should not take the credit for themselves but give credit to the young people; it should not be 'look what we have done for you', but 'look what you have done for yourselves' and 'look what we can do together'".

Active citizenship in schools also poses challenges for staff. At a previous school, Jeremy Cunningham faced strong reactions from colleagues who complained that he "cared more about the students than the teachers; that the students had more rights than responsibilities and that creating opportunities for them to be heard would create indiscipline". From the point of view of staff there is also the question of who will do the work associated with new initiatives. The first Community Day at John Mason, for example, was organised top-down by a member of the senior management team but this created "quite a lot of resistance and resentment". Integrating the Community Day into year groups was much more successful, yet for class teachers already under pressure the time taken to organise 150 pupils to participate in a community project may be time that they feel they simply do not have.

It is perhaps here that the introduction of citizenship to the curriculum faces its greatest challenge. As Jeremy Cunningham highlights, having citizenship as a statutory subject for 11 to 16 year olds "gives it great legitimacy". But this legitimacy needs to be matched by resources; surely many teachers will sympathise with the staff at John Mason who wondered "how could we possibly insert another chunk of content into our already over-stretched programme?" As part of the government's ring-fenced funding from the Standards Agency for the introduction of citizenship, the school received a £3000 grant. However, current provision for citizenship "fades in comparison to other government strategies". Comparing it to the new Key Stage 3 strategy, Jeremy Cunningham adds that "Heads of Year cannot be expected to plan events year after year without proper resources". Although the Department for Education and Skills currently has no plans to do so, a partial solution would be to ring-fence funds for a demarcated citizenship grant each year. Recently, several schools have also begun petitioning the government to be awarded specialist citizenship status.

Through its School Council, reading buddies and its culture of student participation, John Mason School provides examples of some of the initiatives that staff and students can take to bring citizenship out of the classroom. This is crucial to the success of citizenship as a subject. "Without a sense of ownership of the school being omnipresent", comments Jeremy Cunningham, "our students would be unlikely to respond to more abstract political concepts; we need working semi-democratic models in our daily lives". Yet the experience of John Mason is that truly active citizenship in schools demands extra time and money from teachers and budgets already over-stretched. It seems that if we are to see the citizenship curriculum fulfil its potential and reach beyond the classroom, then not only must staff embrace the full implications of active citizenship but the government must match this growing commitment with appropriate resources.

Section II

The Local Community

Schools and Community Participation
Issues for Citizenship Education

Dr Liam Gearon

Reader in Education and Director of the Centre for
Research in Human Rights, University of Surrey Roehampton

We believe that citizenship education will be strengthened and made more
effective where there is an active contribution from the local community
and where public bodies, including local councillors, MPs and MEPs,
voluntary bodies and community agencies such as police and faith groups,
are involved in learning and activities.

Sir Bernard Crick, *'Education for Citizenship and the Teaching of Democracy in
Schools'*

Citizenship Education and Community Participation

The educational trend toward making citizenship explicit is a response to
dramatic changes in the world in which we live over recent decades.
Increased complexity in many aspects of social and cultural, political and
educational life has led to educational initiatives like citizenship. Recent
international research, for example, on wider factors influencing Citizenship
Education (Kerr, 2003) suggests that:

"The last two decades have witnessed a fundamental review of the
concept of citizenship and what it involves in communities across the
world. This review has been brought about by the impact of the rapid pace
of change in modern societies in the realms of political, economic and
social life and the need to respond to this impact. The pace of change is
having significant influence on the nature of relationships in modern
society at a number of levels, including within, between and across
individuals, community groups, states, nations, regions and economic and
political blocs. This period of unprecedented and seemingly relentless
change has succeeded in shifting and straining the traditional, stable

> boundaries of citizenship in many societies. There has been particular
> pressure on the nature of relationships between differing groups in society
> as well as those between the individual and the state. The pressure has
> triggered a fundamental review across societies of the concepts and
> practices that underpin citizenship. (Kerr, 2003)"

A review of Citizenship Education across countries in response to such
dramatic change (Kerr, 2003) reveals a common set of issues and challenges
that the unprecedented pace of global change presents to national educational
systems. These include the rapid movement of people within and across
national boundaries; a growing recognition of the rights of indigenous peoples
and minorities; the collapse of existing political structures and the fledgling
growth of new ones; the changing role and status of women in society; the
impact of the global economy and changing patterns of work and trade on
social, economic and political ties; the effects of the revolution in information
and communications technologies; an increasing global population and the
consequences for the environment; and the emergence of new forms of
community and protest.

Citizenship Education, then, is an active – and at present highly transitional –
response to these challenges. In this, community participation will be at the
heart of any education in citizenship. And genuine participation addresses not
simply the necessary requirement of the Citizenship Order but those
principles that underlie the National Curriculum itself, namely, providing
opportunities for all pupils to learn and achieve, and promoting children's
spiritual, moral, social and cultural development, and preparing them for the
opportunities, responsibilities and experiences of life. (Department for
Education and Employment, 1999)

In setting out what schools are required to teach, the National Curriculum
for Citizenship incorporates active participation with knowledge and
understanding and developing skills of enquiry and communication under the
now familiar headings of knowledge and understanding about becoming
informed citizens, skills of enquiry and communication, and skills of
participation and responsible action. (DfEE, 1999)

In underlining the importance of Citizenship, the Qualifications and
Curriculum Authority stresses how it provides learning opportunities for
pupils:

> "to gain the knowledge, skills and understanding necessary to play an
> effective role in society at local, national and international levels".

In highlighting what this means for pupils, active participation is emphasised
most of all. Citizenship thus:

- helps them to become informed, thoughtful and responsible citizens who are aware of their duties and rights.

- promotes spiritual, moral, social and cultural development, making them more self-confident and responsible both in and beyond the classroom.

- encourages pupils to play a helpful part in the life of their schools, neighbourhoods, communities and the wider world.

- teaches them about our economy and democratic institutions and values; encourages respect for different national, religious and ethnic identities; and develops pupils' ability to reflect on issues and take part in discussions. (QCA, 2001).

Issues in Community Participation

What is my experience of this society?

The final report of the Advisory Group on Citizenship cites an Ofsted inspector as reporting: 'There are few opportunities to develop citizenship, mostly because there is no agreed view of what this entails' (Crick, 1999: 8). But behind this statement is the inevitable potential for multi-faceted, multicultural societies to represent a range of values and even worldviews - shaped by economics, ethnic backgrounds, faith perspectives, gender and political ideologies. Notions of what are the best forms of personal behaviour and the preferred forms of collective responsibility may well vary according to differences in values and worldview. So too will ideas of how individuals and groups within democratic context can effect change and how these should effect change, at all levels - locally, nationally and internationally. As ideas of participation within society contain challenges and tensions, so too will the notion of community participation in citizenship.

Arguably, the best models of Citizenship Education in practice will place emphasis upon a positive experience of the process of community participation. Any citizen in any society will hold a view about his or her experience of living and participating in that society depending upon the quality of this experience. This is not an abstraction. Nor is it a liberal-minded indulgence. Can I express myself freely without fear of repression? Do I have enough to eat? Are the resources of the world really being fairly distributed? Is sustainable development a reality? Does my family face torture, wrongful imprisonment or persecution for religious or political views? Negative responses to these sample questions about the experience of participation will fundamentally affect a person's well-being and sense of what it means to be a citizen in that society. How one defines and prioritises ideas of social and political participation will depend upon values and worldview held (Gearon, 2002).

Does citizenship include me?

Numerous guidance documents from the QCA and Department for Education and Skills also raise issues of inclusion in school and class (see links at www.qca.gov). It is encouraging to see official guidance that makes reference to avoiding gender stereotyping, showing concern for the needs of students with special needs, and recognising the varied learning contexts of refugee and traveller children, among others. The major focus is perhaps understandably on classroom teaching, and much of the advice is explained in terms of attainment. But this approach can mean that the participative element here is neglected. More research will be needed in the early stages of the implementation of Citizenship to monitor and critically engage with questions about the nature of active participation: who participates in school citizenship projects, what form do school councils take, are pupils involved in decision making, what is the extent and range of community projects, and is the focus of participation entirely local or are national and global perspectives on involvement encouraged?

Community participation and responsible action

Advice from the QCA recommends that teachers of sufficient seniority are provided with responsibility for overseeing the implementation of citizenship across the whole school community. When one begins to examine some of the practical issues that arise when implementing active participation for students one can see why. One of the reasons that citizenship requires the involvement of teachers of sufficient seniority, and indeed the involvement of senior management, is that issues of active participation – in citizenship as in any other area of the curriculum – raises issues of pupils' health and safety. This is particularly evident if active participation involves taking groups of pupils – however large or small – beyond school premises or having visitors to the classroom or school.

It is for such reasons that the DfES has issued guidance on safety during school visits and on activities involving active participation. The DfES emphasises that Local Education Authorities now have responsibility for release of school time to allow for training. There are obvious resource implications. As Health and Safety of Pupils on Educational Visits (HASPEV), first published in 1998 suggests: when planning activities involving visits or any aspect of active participation by and with pupils, it is also advisable to contact relevant professional associations, the Government Health and Safety Executive, and related legislative authorities on risk assessment and responsibility. The nature and extent of risk assessment and responsibility will depend upon the nature of the activity. Consult fully with senior managers in the planning of any activity, however minor this might appear. Check that you, accompanying staff, pupils and their parents/ guardians of children are aware of all aspects of the activity.

Dr Liam Gearon

Evaluating School-Community Participation

For effective participation in the community an audit of whole school provision is crucial, revealing what links with community groups are already established and through what subjects. Moreover, an audit can spot gaps and overlap in provision. It can also identify levels and forms of pupil participation. Osler - at the Centre for Citizenship Studies in Education - provides a useful five-stage and developmental model of participative and experiential learning:

- Pupils become aware

- Pupils become more informed

- Pupils develop their understanding

- Pupils develop their own views and opinions

- Pupils takes action (Osler 2001: 12)

It is also important to evaluate. One of the ways to make assessment itself active and participatory is to engage pupils in this process.

Resources are available for schools seeking to increase their participation in the community. One such is Community Partners, an initiative developed in conjunction with the Department for Education and Skills in response to the launch of Citizenship in the National Curriculum. What distinguishes the work of Community Partners is its emphasis upon active participation. The focus is three-fold:

- Directory of community organisations
  Extensive list of groups that can offer support to schools with a targeted search device to suit your pupils' needs

- Case studies and project ideas
  A thematic guide according to key stage subject area of useful, tried and tested approaches to active citizenship

- Guidelines for good practice
  Downloads including:
  - Quick guide to the Context of Community Involvement
  - A Checklist of Success Factors for Community Involvement

The Community Partners initiative also contains a useful 'Checklist of Success Factors for Community Involvement' that could provide a useful working framework for teacher and pupil evaluation for key stage 3 and 4. The downloadable document has six headings:

(1)   The importance of explicit support for community involvement

(2)   The success factors for good practice

(3)   A methodology for active learning in the community

(4)   A checklist for quality community involvement

(5)   A checklist for developing community partnerships

(6)   Celebration and accreditation of pupils' learning and achievements (www.csv.org.uk)

Political Literacy and Social Change: The Need for Research

> "Civic spirit, citizens' charters and voluntary activity in the community are of crucial importance, but individuals must be helped and prepared to shape the terms of such engagements by political understanding and action." (Crick 1998: 10)

One obvious, commonsense question that might be raised in relation to Citizenship, and active participation in the community in particular, is: can Citizenship Education really make a difference? Underpinning the question of active citizenship is the number of areas where the curriculum meets the community - locally, nationally and globally. Here, Kerr (2003) presents four challenges, applying "not just to England but wherever attempts are made to review and strengthen civics or Citizenship Education":

- *The curriculum challenge*
  Issues of definition, how and where Citizenship fits in the curriculum and its relationship to other areas and aspects of the curriculum

- *The community challenge*
  Relatedness of pupils to active citizenship but also their families, their immediate environment, the media and the example of those in public life - how to involve parents, governors and community representatives and support agencies in Citizenship Education in meaningful participation with schools.

- *The global challenge*
  Preparedness for the pace of change in global society.

- *The individual challenge*
  The awareness and participation of the individual in social life.

In planning for active community participation in Citizenship in schools, all of these factors need to taken into account. Active participation takes pupils beyond political literacy into the arena of social and political change.

Yet recent reviews of the research in the field show that the evidence base in a post-Crick and post- National Curriculum context is limited (Gearon 2003). The Evidence for Policy and Practice Information and Co-ordinating Centre (EPPI) is presently (2003) working on a number of evidence-based research projects concerned with citizenship. Such research reviews provide some basic co-ordinates of historic, current and future research in citizenship for practitioners and policy-makers. Since the subject involves wide collaboration within groups and agencies beyond the school community, a major area for future research will be those sectors external to the school that aid and assist the delivery of Citizenship through active participation and wider community involvement – from the financial service sector to the media, from the law and local government to the voluntary sector and NGOs.

References

Crick, Bernard/ QCA (1998) Education for Citizenship and the Teaching of Democracy in Schools (Crick Report), London: Qualifications and Curriculum Authority.

DfEE (1999) The National Curriculum for England: Citizenship, London: Department for Education and Employment and the Qualifications and Curriculum Authority

EPPI (2003, in progress) An international Review of Citizenship Education Research The Evidence for Policy and Practice Information and Co-ordinating Centre (London: EPPI)

Gearon, Liam ed (2002) Human Rights and Religion: A Reader Brighton and Portland: Sussex Academic Press

Gearon, Liam (2003) Citizenship Education: A BERA Professional Research Review London: British Educational Research Association

Kerr, David (2003) 'Citizenship Education in International Perspective', in Gearon, Liam ed. Learning to Teach Citizenship in the Secondary School, London: Routledge.

NFER (2002) England's Results from the IEA International Citizenship and Education Study: What Citizenship and Education Mean to 14 Year Olds, Slough: NFER

Osler, Audrey (2001) Global Citizenship Leicester: Centre for Citizenship Education Studies

Community Action and Young Person Led Participation

Sally Stenton

Programme Manager at the Changemakers Foundation.
She works for the Active Citizens in School (ACiS)
National Pilot in Peterborough and Cambridgeshire

Introduction

In a fast changing and increasingly complex world where young people need preparation to become global citizens, the role of education in simply instilling an existing body of knowledge has been increasingly challenged. Teachers and the institutions in which they operate offer traditions and lessons from the past, but young people hold much that can unlock the future; the learning journey needs to be a partnership between adults and students. This is the essence of the Changemakers approach: placing adults in the role of facilitator and young people and their energy, concerns and curiosity at the centre of the learning process.

Changemakers was founded in 1994 with the aim to develop and promote a young person-led approach to community involvement. The central model involves the following stages;

Young people identify and explore issues in their communities - locally and/or globally.

- They explore their values and aspirations

- They choose an issue or need on which to take action.

- They work in groups to research, plan and carry out their project.

- They review their learning together

- They celebrate their achievements

The DfES funded 'Active Citizens in School National Pilot' has provided the opportunity for testing out the application of this approach in the delivery of

Citizenship Education. Exploring the real practical and logistical challenges of turning theory and vision into practice, it offers a wealth of examples demonstrating the spectrum of activity and the scope for building both entitlement and progression for all students. The model of young person-led action and learning demonstrates how knowledge, understanding and skill can be developed in tandem through an active process. This approach necessitates young people's involvement in enquiry and research and in exploring their own values and aspirations. Knowledge is acquired and built on because the action requires it.

The approach of young person-led action can form an integral element of Citizenship Education and is particularly relevant to the development of greater civic engagement and the promotion of participatory democracy. The challenge for adults is in sharing power by providing a framework that models the democratic process and encourages creativity and leadership by young people. Schools have reported immense popularity of approaches that value young people's ideas, give them responsibility and support them to work in groups on real issues and needs.

Civic Engagement

A key purpose of the Citizenship curriculum is to engage young people in the political process and in making a positive contribution to their community, local and global. The development of the UK Youth Parliament and growing popularity of school councils and youth forums have a part to play, but other approaches are needed in order to engage more than just a minority of young people. Community action is an element of participatory democracy that can motivate and involve young people on their own terms in a way that formal political processes often fail to do. There is a danger of youth councils replicating the non-participatory democracy that is currently failing to engage much of the electorate, rather than embracing the opportunity for young people to apply their creativity and energy to develop new models and approaches and take action themselves. The concept of young people identifying issues and taking action involves a recognition that each person's responsibility and opportunity as a citizen extends beyond the ballot box.

The focus on a progression towards young people initiating and leading projects places their participation at the heart of active citizenship, reflecting the concept of participatory democracy as advocated by David Blunkett, *Civic Renewal: A New Agenda* (June 2003). It also supports the notion that civic engagement involves the encouragement of all people to participate actively and take responsibility for improving their communities - local and global. Positive experience of participation within school becomes the basis for participation in the wider community, providing a vehicle for promoting participatory democracy by creating opportunities for young people to address issues and needs that they themselves have identified. The dialogue with the community is of vital importance and the beneficiaries of the activity need to be involved in the process of reflection, hence developing a relationship of respect and mutuality.

In some schools that are part of the ACiS programme the young person-led approach has been built into the way that citizenship is *taught* and is hence made available to all. At Ken Stimpson School, Year 9 and 10 students do a 4 week module called 'Taking Action' which gives them the opportunity to explore and research needs and issues based on their own interests and concerns and then to develop their own projects out of lesson time if they choose to do so. There is a room devoted to active citizenship for use by young people organizing projects, and young people operate a Youth Bank in school that other young people can apply to for money to run projects. One Ofsted inspector commented that:

> "attitudes to the subject – Citizenship - are very positive and students enjoy the opportunities for discussion, participation and taking action."

At Hinchingbrooke School, the school entered into an effective partnership with Huntingdonshire District Council who had begun to explore how to engage young people and were keen to form partnerships with schools. A group of 10 students volunteered to consult other young people in order to inform the development of the Community Action Plan, setting up the interviews in the form of a Big Brother diary room and interviewing 40 pupils. They collated the findings, identifying key recommendations, and a PowerPoint presentation was given to the Leader of the District Council. He and the Deputy Head of the school were also asked by the young people to respond to questions that had arisen from the project. The project group of young people concluded that

> "young people *do* have opinions about community issues, that they need to be encouraged to express them, and that they raised some very sensible solutions."

There are a number of mechanisms emerging to link projects run by groups of young people with the development of broader democratic structures. For example, at Impington Village College, Cambridgeshire, plans are afoot for 6th formers to set up a 'School Referendum' that will enable young people, school staff and the Parish Council to put forward questions in order to canvas the views of students. Jack Hunt School in Peterborough has established a School Parliament with form reps who promote active citizenship activity in their class and provide a link to the 'cabinet' - alias School Council.

There is also great potential for the involvement of young people in engaging others of similar age and facilitating the young person led approach themselves. For example, the concept of a national 'Action Tank' is being developed by young people in conjunction with Changemakers. Alan Strickland (age 19) is the Development Co-ordinator:

> "Young grassroots activists have key knowledge about the problems facing their communities and 'hands on' experience of the best ways to tackle them. Through a national network of 'Action Advocates' - peer researchers - and an interactive web-site, the Action Tank will allow young activists to share information about the social problems they are tackling and the best ways they've found to do so. This information will be used in national papers and advocacy to identify which key problems are affecting young people and highlight the effective ways that young people themselves have found to deal with them. The Action Tank will draw issues and recommendations for change out of grassroots action and specifically try to engage with disadvantaged and marginalized groups. This moves away from the exclusive bureaucracy of 'youth representation' and moves towards an era where policy is grounded in local realities and all young people are empowered to express their own voice."

In this may lie one key to engaging young people in the world of politics; rather than forming an allegiance to the politics of the past young people are beginning to invent the politics of the future.

Progression and Entitlement

There is a paradox in citizenship that is sometimes expressed in contrasting the individualistic notion of 'good citizens' with the collective notion of 'active citizens'. The experience in the ACiS schools helps to show the important interaction of service and action, that is that each should support rather than contradict the other. This mirrors the desired and necessary balance between rights and responsibilities and makes the crucial connection between emotional literacy and effective action, between the personal and the political. There is a danger, however, that schools which are not open to encouraging young people to express their views and take action will limit themselves to activity that emphasizes adult-led, service activity without reference to participation and political action. Such activity therefore needs to be clearly understood as forming part of a progression. The Advisory group on Citizenship made this very clear when they set out 3 practical objectives:

> "Firstly, children learning from the very beginning self-confidence and social and moral responsible behaviour both in and beyond the class room... Secondly, learning about becoming helpfully involved in the life and

> concerns of their communities… Thirdly, pupils learning about and how to make themselves effective in public life through knowledge, skills and values – what can be called 'political literacy', seeking for a term that is wider than political knowledge alone. (Advisory Group on Citizenship 1998)

To achieve this requires young people to be helped through a development process that is about growing confidence, communication, caring, creativity and political awareness and most of all the motivation to play an active part in their community. Levels of motivation are high when young people are taking responsibility;

> "It is good to be able to lead things, with support from the teacher, rather than just being told what to do." (Male student, age 15)

Young people can thus move from activity that is pre-determined to activity where they begin to take on elements of responsibility and then to ownership and leadership. In order to develop the full repertoire they need the opportunity to engage in a range of activity that will cover the following dimensions:

- Adult-led, young person-centred and young person-led activity

- School based activity and activity in the wider community

- Individual activity and group activity

- Service / helping activity and issue based action

The combined models that are being developed in the ACiS schools help to demonstrate the potential for progression from year 7 through to post-16 education via a combination of entitlement and enrichment activity. The former can provide an overarching framework for all students, a route map to enable them to access wider opportunities and a means by which they can be helped to reflect on their learning. The risk of a system that does not recognize this progression as an entitlement is that it continues to be only the already confident young person who participates and those who have the greatest need to have their voices heard continue to be marginalized. The young people led approach, however, has proved its potential to engage young people who are disaffected, where the action is defined by them, based on their concerns and interests and their views, ideas and solutions are valued. The approach can address the basic need to develop the sense of belonging that is a pre requisite of effective citizenship, as well as the skills for effective action. Take, for example, a group of energetic boys, including some resistant to school, who are given the chance to organize an event. They choose a football tournament for younger students, and a sense of belonging comes from being part of a group with a common purpose and from being part of a school that values their ideas, trusts them to run something themselves and provides the support and encouragement that they need.

It is important, however that Citizenship activity is not confined to specific groups. It is an opportunity for young people to form into groups of people who would not normally work together. When this occurs the enjoyment of working with different people is often one of the positives that is cited by young people. This opportunity to form new groupings makes a valuable contribution to the development of young people as citizens by cutting through the labels and divides, often assumed or imposed.

Facilitation

The idea of young people designing and managing community projects that bring about positive change for themselves and their communities requires a shift of power from the adult facilitator to allow the young people to genuinely control the action. The role of the facilitator is in supporting the action as well as ensuring that there are ample opportunities for young people to plan, develop and review their learning. Teachers playing the role of facilitators do so within the context of organizations that are host to a complex set of power relationships which may not support the new found role of the teacher as enabler. The recognition that learning is enhanced by such approaches gives permission and hence power to this approach, but will inevitably lead to some agitation of the present system and the need to redefine structures and relationships. This includes the logistical issue of the ratio of facilitators to young people; the sustainability of the young person led approach is dependant on this redefinition.

Nonetheless, schools have been enterprising in finding opportunities for facilitators to work with smaller groups. For example, at Sawtry Community College, the Community Challenge Weeks for Year 10 students take place when half the year are on work experience. In other schools volunteers have been involved, and as part of the Social Enterprise model developed by Changemakers, mentors from businesses will play an important role. In some schools Youth Workers work alongside teachers both in and out of lesson time.

A shift of power is implicit also in the combining of formal and informal approaches. This is central to the ACiS pilot and involves teachers and youth workers working together to create a focused, but flexible framework. The sharing of power with young people can be as much an issue for youth workers as teachers. Too little structure can be as disabling as too much and sometimes it is more energising to be in a situation where there is clearly something to fight against than it is to be in an environment that is amorphous or lacking clear boundaries. Combining the best of both formal and informal approaches creates a context where there are clear expectations defined by the group, an environment where creativity and the expression of ideas are encouraged and where it is safe to take risks with opportunities to learn from mistakes, rather than be judged or graded.

Work with a Year 8 class at Sawtry Community College illustrated the positive impact of combining the approaches. Youth workers and the form teacher worked with the young people to map their community and generate ideas for action. The teacher was surprised at the level of maturity and engagement and the Youth Workers found that this attitude continued when they worked with them on their projects - e.g. campaigning for a Skate Park at the Youth Centre.

Conclusion

The Citizenship Curriculum is requiring schools to be the facilitators of increased civic engagement, though in relation to the burgeoning activity around Youth Participation schools are not at the forefront. However, it may be that it is the Citizenship Curriculum - in association with other developments such the National Healthy School Standard and Guidance for schools on participation - that will act as a vehicle for school change, which in turn could impact on the wider political landscape.

If education is to prepare young people to participate in an ever changing world young people need to be helped to define how their world is now, what it may become and to identify what they need to equip them to deal with this. Part of this involves making sense of the world and their role in it and having the opportunities to test out their own effectiveness in different situations, with different groups of people. If schools can help to provide these opportunities to all young people then the impact on them, not just as citizens but as self-motivated learners in the changing world of work, will be significant.

For more details of the Changemakers Pilots, Training packages and Guides for Young People, Facilitators and Developers contact Changemakers at: info@changemakers.org.uk Tel 01458 834767

Youth Act!

Carrie Supple

Project Manager of Youth Act at the Citizenship Foundation

Introduction

Youth Act! is a project which works closely with groups of young people to foster their personal development, social understanding and political empowerment by supporting their initiatives for community change. Already successful in the US[1], where it is run by the charity Street Law, the Citizenship Foundation is intending to adapt Youth Act! into a UK context in the coming year. Initially, we are piloting it with young people in Haringey and Islington, aiming to expand over 3 years to all of London, with the ultimate aspiration of becoming national.

The project responds to growing concern about disaffection from the political process, heightened by a record low turnout in the 2001 General Election with only 39% of 18-24 year olds voting, and the perception of an increasingly violent, divided and uncaring society. Young people are often seen as part of the problem, but our research into youth social action highlighted how many had ideas and a sense of responsibility about changing the world around them.

The Citizenship Curriculum, now compulsory for 11-16 year olds, is an added impetus to the initiative. Aiming to equip young people to take part in public life, the curriculum has three broad strands: social and moral responsibility, political literacy and community involvement. Youth Act! meets requirements across all these areas, but particularly the community and active citizenship element, which many teachers are concerned about fulfilling.

11–18 year olds in Haringey and Islington were asked to submit ideas for tackling a problem in their school or community, such as discrimination, drugs or homelessness. The proposals were required to have defined and achievable goals, addressing identified needs in an innovative way through effecting structural change, such as influencing local authority policy. For example, we would distinguish between volunteering in a homeless shelter - although extremely worthwhile in itself - from campaigning to change the local council budget or policy on homelessness. Youth Act! in the US has found that it is extremely empowering for the young people involved to move beyond community service to making a real impact on public policy.

It will be crucial for the young people to work collaboratively, with the support of an adult mentor, and to have the capacity to be self-sustaining - where goals may not be achieved within the year. We have raised awareness of Youth Act! through contact with schools and youth groups, including publicity, meetings and training, focusing on deprived areas to encourage applications from disadvantaged young people.[2] The project was boosted by securing music artist Ms. Dynamite's endorsement and permission to include her picture on our leaflets and posters. She was the celebrity most young people wanted to be associated with Youth Act!

The pilot schemes

The US experience suggests that in year 1 it is realistic to work closely with around 8 projects, involving at least 30 young people. The steering group selected these, striving to be as inclusive as possible but retaining discretion as to those most likely to benefit from support and to effect community change. These young people will then be supported in realising their projects through developing their citizenship skills, such as communication, campaigning, advocacy, responsible participation, group work and decision-making. We will endeavour to broaden their understanding of local problems in a socio-political context and facilitate contact with a range of external experts. This is intended to kick-start their projects so that they can be sustained independently as appropriate after that time.

For this initial year there were eight successful project applicants for the first phase of Youth Act! in London: these were chosen by a panel of young people and adults. Each group includes 3 - 5 young people and at least one supportive adult - Learning Mentors, youth workers, or teachers.

- Haringey: *Park View Academy*
  Reducing street crime and increase personal safety;
  Northumberland Park School
  Improving the school environment and reducing litter pollution;

- Tottenham *Young Citizens of Today*
  Providing more places for young people to go in the evenings.

- Islington   *Islington Arts and Media School*
                   Developing inter-school performing arts activities to
                   break down conflict
                   Canonbury Project
                   Improving the facilities for young people on the
                   Bentham Estate
                   Central Foundation School
                   Developing the anti-bullying work of the school.

Participants in Youth Act! will benefit from sustained support, including:

- a practical manual on developing community projects.

- a series of training sessions, combining general political awareness,
  community action, specific issues-based learning, skills development
  and opportunities for young people to 'interrogate' external experts,
  such as MPs, community groups, police, local authority councillors and
  officers. The details have been shaped in consultation with young
  people.

- regular contact between the project manager and participants to
  encourage them in their projects and offer advice, as well as being
  available by phone and e-mail.

- peer support through meeting fellow and previous participants to
  share ideas.

- a presentation event for the young people to publicly celebrate the
  progress their projects have made and the skills they have learnt over
  the year.

We are also looking at ways of accrediting the young people's involvement
in Youth Act!, possibly through the ASDAN award or another purpose-built
mechanism. The US experience of Youth Act! and our research into youth
social action in the UK has emphasised the importance of having "supportive
adults pushing us along all the time." We have therefore asked each group to
find a dedicated adult mentor, in addition to the help we can offer.

Youth Act! will be advised by a steering group of external experts, including
young people, LEA advisors, teachers, youth workers, councillors and
representatives of other organisations such as Youth Action.[3] Evaluation of
Youth Act! will be focussing on the extent to which it has met participants'
expectations, broadened their socio-political understanding and encouraged
their ongoing active citizenship. The young people will keep a record of the
progress of their initiatives, including reflection on the usefulness of the training
and support, and their perceived impact on the local community. We will also
use written feedback forms - which can be anonymous - at the end of the
training sessions and encourage the young people to report back on their

progress the following year so that we have a sense of the longer term impact. The steering group will review the project on the basis of these measures, and any more personal ad-hoc feedback, in the summer of each year.

Review for and future roll-out

The steering group's review of the Islington/Haringey pilot will help to inform the detailed shape of Youth Act! in years 2 and 3. This will be crucial in determining how many new boroughs it is realistic to include, the number of projects to support and the staff resource needed. Our expectation is to work with a minimum of 15 groups in at least 4 boroughs in the second year, with the aim that by year 3 we will be able to invite involvement from across London. Through the review process, we will also look at ways to expand the project nationally, developing a sustainable framework to begin to offer Youth Act! elsewhere in the UK from 2005/6.

Notes:

1.   www.youthact.org
2.   Participation will be free so as not to exclude anyone for financial reasons
3.   Previous participants will be involved after the first year

The impetus Awards

Sheila Bloom

Chief Executive Institute for Global Ethics UK Trust

The motto of the pupil council at Kilbowie Primary School in Clydebank is *'They do make a difference'*. The pupils in Kilbowie are very clear as to the reason why the school has a pupil council. Their justification is based on Article 1 of the Human Rights Act that came into force throughout the UK on October 2, 2000:

> "Everyone has the right to freedom of expression. This right shall include freedom to hold opinions and to receive and impart information and ideas without interference by public authority and regardless of frontiers."

The pupil council at Kilbowie came up with the idea that it would help learning and concentration if pupils were allowed to have water to drink throughout the day. This suggestion was put to the senior management team of the school, and it was agreed that it would be necessary to consult pupils, staff and parents. Questionnaires were put together and issued to all pupils in the eldest class, and their parents, and to all members of staff. It was then agreed that class P7 would pilot the project and would be allowed to have water at work, if they wished it, for a three-month trial period. In order to be allowed to participate in the pilot, a pupil had to apply for a water licence

Throughout the trial period, the pupil council monitored the project by checking that the privilege of having water was not being abused. They also prepared a survey to check on pupils' views as to how it was going. Most pupils viewed it a great success. Teachers noted that most pupils had got a water licence and that it was now considered to be a right of P7 pupils. This led to class discussion about rights and responsibilities; whilst recognising that it was a right to have water, they agreed that with this right came some responsibilities – the need to abide by the rules of the licence.

The pupil council met again to decide how to take the project further – in particular into the local community. Various suggestions had been made but it was the pupil council itself that came up with the idea of a consultation with local businesses on their knowledge and use of 'water at work'. Another survey was drawn up and issued. Results indicated that very few businesses allowed their staff access to water at work. The pupil council decided that as this was due to lack of knowledge of the value of 'water at work', it should invite managers into the school for a presentation. This was duly done.

In evaluating this innovative project, the Local Voluntary Panel - one of eight such panels set up to support the schools and youth organisations taking part in the pilot in 2002 - felt strongly that the submission had met all four of the criteria by which entries were to be judged. Projects submitted for the impetus Awards needed to show:

- increased awareness of shared rights and responsibilities

- the underlying values explored and developed in practical and creative ways

- promotion of whole institution involvement

- engagement with the local community

In Kilbowie's case, the concept of rights with responsibilities had been addressed; the whole school had been involved; and there had been engagement with the local community. In addition, a number of the core values underpinning the Human Rights Act – such as mutual respect, honesty and integrity, fairness of treatment, and personal freedom and personal responsibility – had been explored in creative ways.

Kilbowie's project was one organised and managed by the pupil council in the school. Many of the other entries in the pilot scheme – from around 100 schools and 45 youth organisations in England, Northern Ireland, Scotland and Wales – were equally innovative. Representative examples were showcased at a celebratory event at Church House, Westminster, on October 2nd, the Second Anniversary of the launch of the Human Rights Act. Entries ranged from the development of a sensory garden in a special school in north Wales to the introduction of an anti-bullying policy in Northern Ireland, led by young people themselves.

The primary aim of impetus is to encourage young people to explore what our shared values are – and should be - and to help them develop the confidence and courage to put those values into practice in their communities. By promoting and celebrating good practice in values-based approaches to education for citizenship, in the context of the Human Rights Act, the scheme endorses whole school/youth organisation involvement, as well as engagement with local communities, thus fostering social cohesion. A long-term vision for the project is a culture of reciprocity – or of "doing as you would be done by" – throughout the UK, through an increased awareness of rights and responsibilities.

impetus is a free scheme that will run as a rolling programme in England, Northern Ireland, Scotland and Wales, coordinated within each of these nations according to local needs. Local groups - Local Voluntary Panels - are being established to support entrants and help determine representative examples of good practice. impetus will seek to involve young people at every level and will especially reach out to those schools and youth organisations that do not usually participate in award schemes or competitions.

An independent evaluation of the benefits to schools and youth organisations of taking part in the pilot was carried out by the School of Education, Manchester Metropolitan University, and the findings were published in November 2002.

The researchers found that, for the young people taking part in the scheme, impetus had:

- increased their self esteem and personal confidence

- developed their inter-personal, vocational and creative skills

- involved them in active, community-based citizenship

- improved their understanding of citizenship and related themes

- empowered them through recognizing their hard work

In addition, teachers, youth workers and volunteers said that the awards had raised important citizenship issues such as human rights - and responsibilities - community understanding, conflict resolution, and social understanding; and they also highlighted the importance of:

- Interaction: young people and adults working together

- Recognition: for young people, teachers, schools and communities.

- Developmental impact on young people: increased confidence; self-esteem; belief; responsibility; respect for themselves and for others.

Encouraged by these results, the Institute for Global Ethics UK Trust, in a partnership with the Citizenship Foundation, is now engaged in expanding the scheme in a phased regional roll-out throughout the UK. Beginning this autumn – with a formal press launch at the Young Peoples Parliament at Millennium Point in Birmingham on October 2, the third anniversary of the introduction of the Human Rights Act – schools and youth organisations from additional regions in each of the four countries will be encouraged to participate. Key to this expansion is the role of the Local Voluntary Panels (LVPs). LVPs have three main roles to perform: that of promoting the scheme; befriending schools and youth organisations and encouraging them to take part; and in evaluating the submissions.

In fact the research by Manchester Metropolitan University found that:

> "…pupils felt that they had benefited from meeting adults, especially those involved with the Local Voluntary Panels (LVPs)".

It was also felt that visits from LVP members who were outside of the school/youth organisation community:

> "helped to counteract the negative images of schools and young people that dominate much media coverage".

In addition, the LVPs:

> "created a lot of interest and publicity in local communities and among other schools that, along with the awards, led to greater self and external recognition of the work done by the teachers involved".

LVP members have a key role to play in promoting impetus scheme in their areas. They can bring an important and positive external perspective and recognition into schools and youth organisations that can help open up or reinforce contacts with the community in a way that adds real value to citizenship studies. An LVP member's personal role and experiences in the local community are also likely to be relevant to the issues young people are exploring. Equally, LVP members in the pilot scheme, representative of many different sectors within the communities involved, were deeply impressed by the work that they found was taking place. LVP engagement with schools and youth organisations is therefore strongly encouraged, and one of the key features of impetus.

Another core pillar of impetus is its emphasis on creativity. Submissions can be in any form or media. Work presented in the form of visual or performing arts, showing the connections between aesthetic values and ethical values and behaviour, will also be welcome. Submissions during the pilot included a wide variety of presentations, including drama, video, murals, rap, role-plays and many, many more. And whilst a certificate will be given to any school or youth organisation that shows it is exploring and developing shared values in the context of the Human Rights Act, it is also planned to use available funding to enable local artists to be commissioned to produce enduring works of art to mark the school youth organisations' achievement. That commissioning process will best be undertaken by the school or youth organisation in liaison with their Local Voluntary Panel, and is seen as an extension of the engagement with their local community. In the pilot, commissions have included a six foot tall wooden sculpture to stand in the entrance hall, a buddying bench depicting hands and set in a quiet area of the playground, murals for inside and outside, six life-size models of children, and a fabric-based mural on the theme of 'transitions' - to reflect and celebrate work being done with the secondary school's feeder primaries.

Four Country Panels have been established to oversee the scheme in each country, and each will determine how best this should be done according to local circumstances and available funding. impetus is not a competition, but it does seek to celebrate and promote good practice. So we will showcase the examples of good practice locally and nationally, as well as marking each year's achievements at an annual UK celebration. We plan to celebrate the first full year of the impetus on October 2, 2004!

Further information is available by requesting a full pack containing promotion leaflet, Guidance for Schools and Youth Organisations and a Local Voluntary Handbook from:

Institute for Global Ethics UK Trust
3-4 Bentinck Street
London W1U 2EE

Nobel Civitatis

Liz Byrne

Head of Religion and Ethics and Coordinator of
Citizenship, Key Stage 4 at the Nobel School in Stevenage

Citizenship is ultimately not just about understanding, not even about
attitudes, but about *action*; about achieving change for the better in the
wide world, starting in the classroom, but hopefully going outside it, and
infusing a person's entire life and the many communities in which they
will move.

David Bryer, Director of Oxfam GB

The Nobel School in Stevenage, a new town, is a vigorous and humane
learning community in which high achievement and creativity are the
expectation and the norm. We are linked with the University of
Hertfordshire as one of eighty-two training schools in the country. Before a
Citizenship Curriculum was introduced, along with many other schools, Nobel
already encouraged the knowledge and skills essential to active citizenship
through students' roles and responsibilities within the school and beyond,
acknowledging that responsibility needs to be learned and practised. We were,
in the sixties, one of the first schools to have students on the governing body.

"I have enjoyed helping to improve my school"

Beginning with the day-to-day organization of the school itself, students are
involved in almost every area of school life, starting at the very top. Appointing
a new head teacher this year, for example, students entered into dialogue
about school leadership and their perceived needs as they interviewed
prospective candidates.

"The pupil panel was formed as a means of interviewing applicants for these people were applying for a high responsibility role within the school. Therefore it was important for pupils to have their say, since we are going to be affected directly by the decision.

Two pupils out of every year were picked – one boy and one girl. There was then a meeting where everyone was told what was going to happen. My thoughts of the whole experience were that it was extremely worthwhile and interesting. It made me feel as if I had helped the school in some way. Overall I would love to do it again."

Jonathan, Year 8

"My question was "Do you think students should help run the school?" After we questioned them all, the student panel spoke to the teacher [teacher governor] and discussed who we thought suitable, and numbered them, one being the highest. We all liked Mr. B."

Georgina, Year 8

Teacher and taught together make the teaching and through a Partners in Learning initiative students are trained as observers in lessons and are allocated to a member of staff. After a number of lesson observations they give constructive feedback to teachers using a range of agreed criteria. The project has been running for two years, and two sets of students have been trained as observers. This year twenty-eight students and six members of staff were involved. In the process of evaluation student comments include:

"The class soon forgot that I was there and so did the teacher so I could see the class in their normal atmosphere."

"I have enjoyed learning new things and helping to improve my school."

"I have enjoyed the opportunity to watch teachers in a different light. This made me appreciate the other things that teachers have to take into account as well as teaching the academic work."

Teachers also found the experience beneficial:

"The training meant that students approached the project with very mature attitudes and they were competent when carrying out observations."

"It was nice to know that I'm doing things right!"

This project led to student involvement and presentations at several conferences including the Student Voice Launch of the National College for School Leadership. They have gained in self-esteem knowing they have contributed directly to improvement in teaching and learning in their school and they feel trusted. As Francis Bacon wrote:

"the greatest trust between man and man [sic] is the trust of giving counsel".[1]

Working with Peers: from "I-I" to "I-Thou"

The bedrock of our school, its discipline and learning, is the Respect for All policy to which every student contributed at its formation through tutor group representatives at School Council. The impact of the policy is felt every moment of the school day, in everything we say and do we give power.

Individual attainment needs to go hand-in-hand with collective belonging in a healthy school, especially where the wider society is geared to performance and results. As Jonathan Sacks wrote, metaphorically, we need to be bilingual with a first language of shared citizenship, and a second language of personal identity, which is a matter of family and history[2]. Most noticeable to visitors to our school is its warm atmosphere, welcoming to all. That students are encouraged to be responsible for the welfare of each other is vital for in the world beyond the school gates students are often encouraged to be more conscious of legal rights than human responsibilities.

Students at Nobel can volunteer to be Helpliners, sixth-formers who actively listen, offer a helping hand, advice or shoulder to cry on for younger students who can 'drop-in' during any lunchtime. Helpliners receive training from a deputy head and the school counsellor. Frontliners, students in Years 9 and 10, are a new branch of Helpliners, also trained by the school counsellor, who act as mentors or 'buddies' to new Year 7 students from September as well as to students in years 8 and 9.

Another democratic process, Circle Time, a well-known approach in primary schools, is being piloted in a Year 9 tutor group. Students take process and rules extremely seriously, demonstrate mutuality, empathy and amazing openness, and ask for more frequent sessions. Research has shown that quality circle time can help secondary schools promote the aims of social inclusion, positive behaviour and citizenship.[3]

Sixth-form volunteers run the Key Stage 3 Study Centre, where students can choose to study during lunchtimes and after school, and are responsible for its administration, opening hours, rotas and, to a large extent, discipline. Incidentally, Nobel views discipline as students following someone whom they respect rather than as imposed; interestingly the word has the same root as disciple. Sixth-formers are also attached to Year 7 tutor groups during term time and to different year groups during activities week when the whole school is off-timetable.

Recent national emphases on literacy, language for learning, and thinking skills are no-where used to greater effect than in students voicing and acting on their concerns, for once you name something, you have power over it to influence change, and this is surely what citizenship is about and what can make Citizenship lessons that spill-over beyond the classroom so enjoyable. We encourage students to voice concerns and to be involved in decision-making in the school community through their school council.

The Nobel School Council is a mechanism that enables all students, through tutor group representatives, to take part in the day-to-day organization and running of the school. It comprises year-group councils, each of which is organised, chaired and run by two members of the senior student team, sixth-formers, with a senior student co-ordinating the whole. The main concerns this year have been cashless vending and lunchtime catering, litter and the environment, the choice of charities to support and the organization of charity events for each year group. The whole council met with representatives from the catering firm to ensure that it saw things from the students' perspective, to air grievances and suggest improvements.

Representatives from the whole School Council recently attended the Stevenage Youth Forum from which some students will attend the National Youth Forum in Liverpool. We also hold a mock election at the time of a General Election and Sally was a candidate in 1997:

> "I learned first-hand the pressure of presenting a political party to people be they cynical, apathetic or interested. This enhanced my interest in the political views of the day, and I think encouraged others to follow current affairs."

> Sally Brooks, former Nobel student

A further point is that our school is unique in this country in having permission from the Nobel Institute to use the name Nobel, in the hope that it serves as "a reminder of a great man and a symbol of the ideas he stood for"[4]. Tutor groups are named after Nobel laureates, one of whom, Amartya Sen, presently the Master of Trinity College, Cambridge, visited us. He received the prize for his work in welfare economics.

> "When asked about his solutions to famine, the Professor said, 'Foremost, it is necessary to dissociate famine from low food supply, because famine is still in countries that have food'. He went on to explain that the key to eliminating famine is democracy, because famine does not occur in democratic nations. 'In democracy, it is the government's fear of criticism from opposition and the media, which motivates improvements'"

> Nathan and Sam, Year 10 (Nobel News, July, 2000)

There's national and global citizenship! Thus, from day one in Year 7, a student is linked, through their tutor group, to a Nobel laureate, a citizen, who has endeavoured and achieved great things for society, often global society. In annual laureate assemblies we emphasise that a current student could be a laureate for research cited by Michael Barber, which suggests that such links, through a school's name, inspire students. And as Basil Hume wrote,

> "All educators have the task of helping to form young people with their dreams and hopes still alive . . . equipped to think and act morally."

In these many ways, through an inspirational school name and student participation in decision-making at almost every level, we create together a trustworthy environment where students and staff feel safe and respected: Nobel is part of the Hertfordshire Well-Being project and research suggests a high overall well-being measure amongst all Nobel staff.

'Only connect': contributing to local priorities

Students coming into Nobel relate to the local community mainly through shopping and it is our aim that they move beyond *tesco ergo sum* to broaden experience of the immediate locality and expand their horizons. Sixth-formers, therefore, volunteer in health and social care at local care homes, nurseries and schools, while through the Millennium Volunteer scheme they work at the Citizens' Advice Bureau and at a local hospital. They annually run a successful cabaret to raise money for local charities. In lessons other than citizenship, in philosophy and ethics for example, students in Years 10 and 11 host visits from carers and residents of a local hostel for the homeless to which, sadly, some of our students have had to turn in times of crisis. The Respect for All policy is especially pertinent in these circumstances. Our school council also decided to adopt a linked rehabilitation centre as a recipient of fund-raising for charity.

Students in Year 9 designed and executed a vibrant mural for a local community centre through a joint initiative with Stevenage Borough Council's Community Development team, a safety project to combat the graffiti problem. The community development officer commented:

> "The talent displayed from these kids far superseded my hopes and the quality of their work is astounding. This is definitely the type of community action that we will encourage."

Courtney Giles[5]

Students will also participate in The PUKKA (Peer Understanding, Knowing, Knowledge and Attitude) Project, a series of workshops looking at crime in the community. The project's aim is to produce a motion picture, the first time in British film history that a motion picture has been directly linked to education. The resulting film, packaged as a DVD with an interactive teaching pack, will be offered to every secondary school in the country. Young people will debate a number of their concerns, such as health, drugs, and poverty and will offer constructive solutions from their experience of growing up in a new town. TV celebrities, including some from Eastenders, will talk about their work and take part in the discussion.

We have many other local links: students have practised investigative journalism and contributed to a local newspaper, they have loaned GCSE artwork for stimulus material to a local primary school and have contributed to a local art exhibition. Work experience takes place in the local community while every December, Year 10 drama students invite all Year 6 students from a local primary school to a performance of their work, generally panto-style! Citizenship involves fun and celebration too. In these and other ways Nobel links with the local Stevenage and Hertfordshire communities.

Design, dig, weed, compost, plant, deadhead, pot and water ...

Some Year 10 students have been involved for the past three years in designing, digging and maintaining an RE Garden at the school that has won several awards and contributed to Stevenage's success at Anglia in Bloom. Several people doubted that the garden could survive groups of unsupervised teenagers during weekends but our experience is that trust is rarely misplaced. Last month student gardeners hosted sixty children from a neighbouring primary school, explaining the symbolism of their own 'feast of life' flowerbeds. They also took part in a film of the garden for the Hertfordshire Gardens Trust that will be distributed to each school in the county. Kieran, a student, says:

> "It's good to create a place where you can go to find peace and do some thinking".

During activity days students also care for the Nobel Memorial Garden.

Celebrate and remember: links with national occasions and priorities

Through assemblies and within subject areas we connect with, and explore, national and international moments, and occasions from the London Marathon to Human Rights Day, Holocaust Memorial Day, the International Decade for a Culture of Peace and Non-Violence for the Children of the World (2001-2010).

At a national level, classes of Year 10 students contributed to research into citizenship for the now defunct Council for Education in World Citizenship (CEWC) while a small group representing Years 8 to 11 attended a CEWC human rights conference:

> "I especially liked the way they didn't have just anyone giving these talks. For example, when we were spoken to about disabled people's rights, a disabled person actually talked to us ... I realised that we don't only have to talk to get our opinions and feelings across, we can use many different techniques, for example, music, drama, art and many more."
>
> Candice, Year 11

When democracy flourished in fifth-century Athens, culture was sung and danced with a voice and seat for everyone. Following this conference, Jeremy, a Year 8 student, wrote a "comprehensive, well-informed contribution" about his vision of the world and concerns[6] that led directly to some students attending Youthvoice Worldwide at the Children's Rights International Conference at Westminster Hall. The first I knew of it was when Jeremy e-mailed to ask if I could arrange an afternoon off and for the telephone numbers of other students so that he could arrange transport. Initiative will out!

International links: amazing similarities and glorious differences

Nobel students visit the Somme and Auschwitz with the history department, and France and Germany on MFL trips. All students have the opportunity, through the town-twinning of Stevenage with Kadoma, Zimbabwe, to correspond with a penpal and a few students have maintained this link for seven years. On an In-Depth study day we involved all sixth-formers with staff from Amnesty International (AI) and UNHCR to investigate the refugee experience. Through Dan Jones of AI we had the most amazing simulations. We also invited students from a school in Luton to participate, some of whom were asylum seekers. Much formal and informal learning took place for staff and students. We have an Amnesty International group at Nobel:

> "We wrote letters to, and about, prisoners of conscience and attended the National Youth Conference. Here we discovered the plight of people in other parts of the world from other cultures. Our view of the world was broadened, showing us the bigger picture of life today."
>
> Sally Brooks, graduate

We expand students' horizons with speakers expert in their fields: the head teacher of a local independent school, a Muslim barrister who wears a veil,

Bruce Kent (Movement for the Abolition of War and UN Reform), Gary Younge (assistant editor, The Guardian) who grew up in Stevenage, Patrick Younge (BBC Sport, Director of Programmes) and Tim Radford (science editor with The Guardian). In our experience, speakers value the opportunity of speaking to and with young people, knowing that the future is in their hands.

In a MORI poll commissioned by the Development Education Association amongst four thousand 11-16 year-olds in 2000, 81% of young people thought they needed to understand global issues to make choices about how to live. This concern is reflected at Nobel where students were outraged at the conditions of workers in factories working for Nike and GAP in Indonesia and several letters were fired off to Cadbury's, including some by the most reluctant of writers, reminding them of their Quaker origins, when information surfaced about child cocoa pickers in west Africa.

To conclude, we know too well from DfEE guidance that we only scratch the surface of citizenship in action, but we dare to hope, through students' freshness of ideas, their involvement in our school and wider community, and the knowledge that they make a difference, that we have offered them the opportunity to develop the knowledge, skills and values to start on the road to lifelong active citizenship: responsible for their actions, outraged by social injustice, and understanding that where a law is unjust, protest is a duty. I'm reminded of the words of Stewart Sutherland, formerly Her Majesty's Chief Inspector of Schools, who suggests the following test to describe an educated person, but which we could also use to describe a good citizen. Imagine that you are wrongly accused, you go to court and there, as Chairman of the Jury, is Jane Bower, that student in Year 11 whom you taught. Do you feel confident? That is the test! The last words go to a former student - who is now a member of a political party[7]:

> All of these projects [candidate in a mock election, Amnesty International activities and taking elderly people shopping} made my wider education make more sense and broadened my horizons. School is about more than simply passing exams. I am looking forward to a career in journalism and part of that is because of the valuable citizenship experience I gained during seven years at Nobel.
>
> Sally Brooks

Liz Byrne

Notes:

1.	Francis Bacon, Essays XX, Of Counsel
2.	BBC World Service Interview: People and Politics, 16 November, 2001.
3.	All Round Success, registered charity no. 1064740, undated.
4.	Letter from the Nobel Institute, Stockholm, May, 1961
5.	'Stevenage Chronicle', September, 2002, p.6
6.	Bibi Small, Centre for International Co-operation
7.	Personally, I'd like to acknowledge OXFAM, Amnesty International and Community Service Volunteers. La lutta continua!

Section III

Political Participation

Politically Alienated or Apathetic?
Young People's Attitudes Towards Party Politics in Britain

Matt Henn & Mark Weinstein

The Nottingham Graduate School for Social & Policy
Research, Nottingham Trent University

Abstract

Following the outcome of the 2001 General Election, when the numbers of
abstainers outweighed the numbers of Labour voters, much attention has been
focussed upon the state of British democracy, and how to enthuse the electorate -
and in particular young people, of whom 61 percent chose to stay away from the
polling stations. While the government is exploring ways to make the whole process
of voting easier - with ideas such as voting over the telephone and the internet - it
may be failing to tackle the real problem. The main challenge is that many young
people appear to find the business of politics uninviting and irrelevant to their
everyday lives. This paper examines data derived from a nationwide survey of 705
attainers — young people who are eligible to vote for the first-time and who have
only limited experience of formal politics. The findings from the study reveal that
these young people are not as apathetic when it comes to 'politics' as conventional
wisdom would have us believe. Instead a picture is emerging of a British youth keen
to play a more active role in the political process, but who appear to be sceptical of
the way the British political system is organised and led, and are turned off by politicians and the political parties.

Introduction

The study of young peoples' engagement with the political process - and
in particular of their attitudes towards party politics - is an under-
researched topic. The significant work completed in this area is either
relatively old (e.g., Jennings 1960; Layton-Henry 1973), limited to a small
number of case studies (e.g., Bhavnani 1991; White, Bruce and Ritchie 2000),
or is based upon the analysis of small sub-samples of young people taken from
samples of the general voting-age population (e.g., Heath and Park 1997; Park

2000). Furthermore, such research tends to focus on the more general field of young people and politics, although typically, this does not give specific or detailed attention to party politics. Our research study aims to fill this gap by providing a detailed investigation into the attitudes of young people towards political parties, and examining more general questions about the degree of support that exists for democratic institutions and processes across the country. This is important, given that policy makers are becoming increasingly concerned about the lack of engagement that young people appear to have with politics in Britain. The main purpose of this study is therefore to examine whether there is a crisis of democratic legitimacy in Britain, in terms of the attitudes of young people toward political structures, institutions, and players - especially the political parties.

Research Design

The data is derived from a nationwide study of the political attitudes of attainers - young people eligible to vote in an election for the first time. We conducted a postal questionnaire survey of 705 young people that included a mix of both closed and open-ended questions. In order to generate our responses, we used a random sampling method, with respondents drawn from the electoral register.

Results

Our results are organised under headings which allow us to examine the extent of young people's understanding of and engagement with politics, the degree to which they feel that there are opportunities open to participate meaningfully in political affairs, their views on the democratic process and the key political players - political parties and professional politicians - and what they consider might be done to make politics more inviting to young people.

Political engagement

Our research reveals evidence that far from being apolitical and apathetic, young people are interested in political issues. When asked about politics in general, 56% of respondents replied that they had some or more interest in the topic - which compares with 13% who had none at all - and nearly half (48%) said that they were interested in the General Election held in June 2001 - only 17% had no interest at all. Furthermore, we found that a majority (54%) considered that they would discuss politics with friends and family in the future.

By combining the data from a number of questions we were able to derive a 'political interest' variable, which we then tested against a number of key socio-demographics in the study. Staying on in full-time education clearly has a significant impact on young people's interest levels, with 47% of those still in full-time education saying that they are 'very' or 'somewhat interested', compared to just 34% of those who left education at the statutory school leaving age. Those with either educational or work-related qualifications are far more likely to be interested in politics (44% very or somewhat interested) compared to those who lack any such qualifications (12%). Gender and ethnicity are also important factors, with young men displaying more interest in politics than young women, and those respondents who classified themselves as white, demonstrating lower levels of interest in politics than their ethnic minority counterparts. The data reveal that young people from manual, unskilled or working class backgrounds are considerably less likely to express an interest in politics than their contemporaries who come from middle or higher social class backgrounds. And where people live appears to have an impact on their interest in political matters. In particular, young Londoners would appear to be the most engaged group with 51% being classified as interested as opposed to just 32% of Welsh and 33% of Scottish people respectively.

As a further indicator of their level of political engagement, we asked an open question – "In your opinion, what is the single most important issue at the moment?". Figure 1 is based upon a re-working of this data. We coded respondents' written answers to this question into themes that seemed to capture the essence of young people's main issue priorities. It suggests that their agenda is a broad one that embraces a wide spectrum of concerns. Contrary to perceived wisdom that young people have a distinctive 'alternative politics' agenda that sets them apart from older adults, the data indicate that their outlook, at least on the surface, is remarkably similar. Nearly half of our sample prioritised concerns over the public services, the largest group mentioning health as the issue of single most importance to them (28%), with others giving precedence to education (14%) and transport (4%). A fifth (19%) of respondents mentioned traditional 'materialist' issues - economic matters, Europe, crime and law and order - as their first choice, indicating a preoccupation with mainstream concerns.

However, an examination of the actual data suggests that in important ways, the perspective that young people bring to some of these issues is at times quite specific – certainly when contrasted with the Westminster discourse. Thus, on the issue of education, young people are less inclined to engage with matters concerning quality, standards and league tables, than they are to express anxieties about the financial implications of taking a university course and with possible student hardship.

Figure 1: Issues of Most Concern

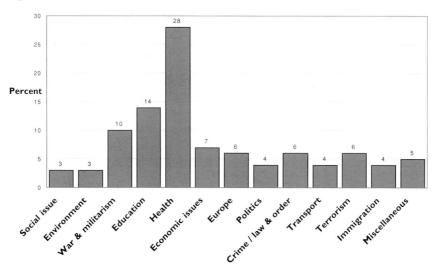

Overall, these results seem to run counter to popular thinking that young people are dismissive of 'Politics'. British youth do profess an interest in the world of political issues and current affairs, and in particular demonstrate an engagement with a variety of political issues. This perhaps belies the characterisation of young people as politically apathetic.

Political knowledge, power and influence

Crucially, although young people express an interest in matters political, they do not feel that they are sufficiently knowledgeable or intellectually equipped to understand 'Politics'. A majority of respondents (53%) stated that they didn't know enough about what is going on in Politics, and a similar number (53%) lacked confidence that they were adequately well-informed about political parties when it comes to deciding how to vote in election. Over half (55%) concluded that they found it difficult to understand what goes on in government and politics. This data suggest that for whatever reason, the message about British political life and political affairs is not being effectively communicated to young people. As a consequence, young people are not particularly well resourced, intellectually, to make informed decisions about politics - this may well help to account for their apparently low rates of participation in formal politics.

Furthermore, the data from our survey indicate that young people do not feel that there exist meaningful opportunities open to them to influence the political scene. Indeed, an overwhelmingly large majority of respondents

considered that they had little or no influence on politics and political affairs -
82%, compared to only 3% who felt they had any influence at all. Comparing
the percentages of those who agreed with those who disagreed on a number
of statements concerning this matter, the data reported in Table I reveal that
attainers felt relatively powerless, politically. They consider that government
does not treat them fairly, and is deaf to their concerns and unresponsive;
consequently, trying to actively engage with and influence government is perceived to be a waste of time.

Table I: Perception of political influence

	Agree %	Disagree %
The government generally treats young people fairly.	23	42
There is a big gap between what young people expect out of life and what we actually get.	64	12
Young people like me have no say in what the government does.	62	21
There aren't enough opportunities for young people like me to influence political parties.	71	7
Being active in politics is a good way to get help for me and my family.	15	41
It takes too much time and effort to be active in politics and public affairs.	36	30

Confidence in the democratic process

Despite feelings of general political powerlessness, young people do appear
to have faith in the democratic process itself, and are generally supportive of
the notion of elections. As Table 2 indicates, when questioned about elections,
young people claim a general attachment to and confidence in the democratic
process.

Table 2: Support for the Democratic Process

	Agree %	Disagree %
All things considered, most elections are just a big waste of time and money.	24	49
Having regular elections forces politicians to listen carefully to public opinion.	51	27
I feel/would feel a sense of satisfaction when I vote.	44	22
I would be seriously neglecting my duty as a citizen if I didn't vote.	43	32
I would only vote in an election if I cared who won.	47	30

The data reveal that gender, ethnicity and qualifications held showed no discernible relation to one's attitudes to elections. However, social class exerted considerable influence - those from manual, unskilled or working class backgrounds are significantly less likely to believe in the electoral process than their counterparts from middle class and higher class backgrounds. Staying on in full-time education clearly has a positive impact on young people's attitudes towards the electoral process, with 59% of 'stayers' exhibiting a strong belief in elections, compared with only 41% of those who are no longer in full-time education. There are also some noticeable regional differences, with those young people living in the London area much more likely to express belief in the electoral process (65%) than their counterparts in Wales (42%) or Scotland (48%). This is perhaps surprising, given that both Wales and Scotland were provided with their own additional tier of regional government in 1999.

Whilst young people broadly consider that elections do matter, they also recognise that elections as a method of democratic participation are limited, and they are sceptical that the outcomes from elections are positive. For instance, a large majority (60%) claimed that elections don't really change anything, and almost twice as many (44%) disagreed than agreed (28%) that by voting they could really help to change the way that Britain is governed. Young people were just as likely to agree (42%) as disagree (36%) that elections help to keep politicians accountable for the promises they make. The data suggests that almost 4 out of 10 young people disagreed that this key principle of representative government actually works in practice. This is a stark indictment of the ability of the political system to win the confidence of young citizens.

Perception of political parties and professional politicians

This guarded position that young people take in relation to the outcomes of elections, appears to be driven by a deep-seated scepticism towards those political parties and politicians who vie for their votes and for political office. Our results show an apparent disconnection from party politics.

Attainers have a relatively low level of party identification (28%, compared to those 59% who report that they do not identify with a political party). Perhaps not surprisingly therefore, nearly all (89%) stated that they would not be prepared to give money to a political party, nor would they be prepared to work for a political party in an election campaign (84%). Only 2% reported membership of any of the political parties.

As Table 3 demonstrates, young people appear to hold deeply sceptical views of political parties and of elected politicians, and of the way that they conduct their activities.

Table 3: Perception of political parties and professional politicians

	Agree %	Disagree %
There is often a big difference between what a party promises it will do and what it actually does when it wins an election	87	3
Political parties are more interested in winning elections than in governing afterwards	69	13
The main political parties in Britain don't offer voters real choices in elections because their policies are pretty much all the same	48	22
Political parties do more to divide the country than unite it	41	24
Political parties spend too much time bickering with each other	76	9
In elections, political parties don't tell people about the really important problems facing the country	50	21
Political parties aren't interested in the same issues that concern young people	59	10
Parties are only interested in people's votes, not in their opinions	65	14
Those elected to parliament soon lose touch with people	59	12

Furthermore, the majority of survey respondents perceive political parties to be remote and incapable of effectively connecting with young people. Respondents were almost twice as likely to agree (44%) than disagree (26%) with the statement that it's embarrassing when the parties try to appeal to young people during election campaigns. Only a small fraction (7%) felt that political parties are good at listening to young people's concerns and then responding to them positively (while 63% disagreed). In addition, the largest group (39%) stated that they considered that Governments do not really care what young people like me think (26% are in disagreement).

The data indicate that all bar one of the groups in the study had a uniformly negative view of the political parties – people did not discriminate on the basis of their gender, ethnicity, social class, region of the country in which they lived, or educational qualifications held. The only differences noted were that those remaining in full-time education demonstrated less aversion to the political parties than those no longer in education.

Re-connecting young people: the challenge for political parties

So what might be done to reverse young people's antipathy to the political parties and professional politicians? The responses from an open question provide certain clues. These were typified in the following answers, which signalled very clearly that the main challenge was for the parties to reach out to young people in a direct, meaningful and non-patronising way:

- "I believe they should inform young people about what's going on. I think a lot of people like me have absolutely no idea about what's going on. The parties should talk to us and explain what they believe is right. Teenagers don't bite!"

- "Stop pretending they care about us and genuinely care. Rather than being fake with us, they could genuinely regard our opinions as important as middle class 40 year olds."

- "I detest cheap stunts – like wearing baseball caps or being an Oasis fan – but simply believe members of political parties should meet young people and listen to and take on board their views and concerns."

By categorising these open responses and conducting a quantitative analysis of the data, Figure 2 indicates that over six in ten attainers consider that the political parties should do more to connect with young people, by making direct contact (26%), listening to young people (21%), and providing clearer information about their programmes and policy positions (10%) – and in a less mystifying and more engaging manner (5%). Clearly, for young people to be brought back into the democratic fold, political parties will need to reflect seriously on how they approach them in the future.

Figure 2: The challenge for political parties?

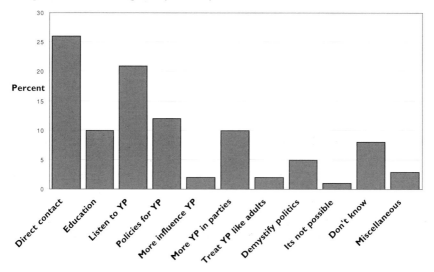

Summary

We have found through this research project that young people in Britain are sufficiently interested in political affairs to dispel the myth that they are apathetic and politically lazy – they have a clear interest in a range of political issues. Furthermore, there is a civic orientation amongst the young to the democratic process: representative democracy is generally seen to be a very good thing. Yet, we can find no evidence from our study that young people consider that the democratic process is open to them, or responsive to their needs. And those charged with conducting Politics on their behalf – the political parties and professional politicians - are perceived to be self-serving, unrepresentative, and unresponsive to the demands of young people.

Perhaps not surprisingly, the data indicate that there is no uniform youth approach to politics in Britain. Differential effects can be observed in this study in relation to region, gender, ethnicity and social class. However, the strongest impact on young people's attitudes towards politics can be traced back to young people's educational experience. Most importantly, staying on in full-time education appears to engender higher levels of participation in the political system.

The main 'policy' conclusion that we must draw from these findings is that if this generation is to become more politically engaged, then the main political parties must take a more positive and proactive approach in their attempts to connect with young people. This group are much more likely to respond to approaches from the political parties that are more direct, participative and transparent, in which it is possible for young people to gauge the extent to which their voices have been heard, listened to, and acted upon.

References

Bhavnani, K.K. (1994) Talking Politics: A Psychological Framing of Views from Youth in Britain (Cambridge: Cambridge University Press).

Bynner, J., and Ashford, S. (1994) 'Politics and Participation: Some Antecedents of Young People's Attitudes to the Political System and Political Activity', European Journal of Social Psychology, 24 (2), pp.223-236.

Heath, A., and Park, A. (1997) 'Thatcher's Children?', in R. Jowell et al (eds.) British Social Attitudes: The 14th Report. The End of Conservative Values? (Aldershot: Ashgate).

Jennings, I. (1960) Party Politics: Appeal to the People (Cambridge: Cambridge University Press).

Layton-Henry, Z. (1973) Political Youth Organisations in Britain: A Comparative Study of the Young (Unpublished PhD, Birmingham University).

Park, A. (2000) 'Young People and Political Apathy', in R. Jowell, J. Curtice, A. Park and K. Thompson (eds.) British Social Attitudes: the 16th Report. Who Shares New

Labour Values? (Aldershot: Ashgate).
Russell, A., Fieldhouse, E., Purdam, K., and Kalra, V. (2002) Voter Engagement and Young People (London: The Electoral Commission).
White, C., Bruce, S. and Ritchie, J. (2000) Young People's Politics: Political Interest and Engagement Amongst 14- to 24- year-olds (York: York Publishing Services).

Youth Participation in Politics
A Glance at Norway

Martin Bratt

Member of the Central Board of the Association of
Norwegian Students Abroad (ANSA)

Context

As a parliamentary monarchy Norway's political system is similar in some ways to Britain's but is marked also by some substantial differences. It has three administrative levels - national, regional and local. Elections are held every two years, with national (parliamentary) elections every four years - last elections were in 2001 - and local and regional elections every four years - last elections were in 1999. The voting age is 18 and, like Britain, voting turnout among young people is considerably lower than among the population as a whole. Nevertheless in the parliamentary elections of 2001, 55.7% of people between 18 and 21 voted and 57.0% of those between 22 and 25 voted, compared to a national average of 77.2%. In 1997 the figures were 58.9% for those between 18 and 21, 65.7% for those between 22 and 25, and 81.3% for the population as a whole. Women have a slightly higher turnout than men.[1]

Youth Politics

There are eight parties represented in the Norwegian Parliament. Six of these have independent youth wings, and one - the Progress Party - has a semi-independent youth wing. Norwegian party politics is very stable; of the current eight parties represented in Parliament, the Coast Party - with only one MP - was founded in the 1990's, one was founded in the 1970's, another one in the 1960's, and all the other parties have existed since before the Second World War. Many youth wings also have a long history, the Young Liberals being the oldest with a history dating back to 1909.

Among the parties represented in Parliament, only the Coast Party does not have a youth wing. The other parties have solid, well functioning and stable youth wings, with the partial exception of the Progress Party, whose youth wing is relatively weak in comparison with the size of the mother party. The Progress Party is also the only party whose youth wing is not fully independent, as its decisions can be revoked by the central board of the mother party.

In Norway, students' unions are less obviously politicised than in Britain, and although some parties have separate students' organisations, most students who participate in party politics stick with the youth branches of the political parties. Norwegian students' unions are apolitical, and tend to have internal factions that represent different opinions on student issues. Only the Labour Party has a well established students' organisation working within the students unions.

Membership and Party Funding

Membership statistics of Norwegian youth parties are not entirely reliable. There are no centralised statistics, and different organisations use different criteria to determine membership. However, rough estimates indicate that at least 10 000 people under the age of 26 pay their membership fee to Norwegian youth parties every year, and that the largest ones have between 2500 and 3500 members. This compares favourably with Britain, given that the population of Norway is under a tenth of Britain's.

The funding of political parties is rarely straightforward, and the financing of political youth organisations has been a controversial issue in Norway. Following a major scandal in the mid-1990's, where political youth parties were found to have exaggerated their membership lists in order to receive extra funding, several important figures were sentenced to short terms in prison. Partly as a consequence of this, the rules for funding were changed. Until then, youth parties had been funded like other youth organisations, based on membership and on proven activities. Under the new system, implemented from 1996, youth parties receive money from national and local authorities based on the electoral performance of their mother parties. Under this scheme, the amount of money a youth party receives per member varies enormously. Large and active youth parties whose mother parties receive few votes are penalised, whereas the youth branch of a big party will receive a huge amount of money regardless of the number of people involved there. This system has also been criticized, but so far there is no talk of change.

Participation

In general, participation in youth politics is fairly common in Norway.

Although only the minority of young people actually adhere to youth parties and take an active part in organisational work, youth parties are well established, and participation is generally well regarded. The two major youth parties, affiliated to the Labour and Conservative Parties, are well known among most young people and get significant media coverage. Leaders of youth parties are regularly invited to participate in debates on television or the radio, and they are often among the most well known figures of a political party. Participation in party politics is well regarded by schools and teachers. High school students in Norway have the opportunity to count organisational work like party politics as school credits, an initiative taken to encourage youth participation. Some of the larger schools have local branches of youth parties; these have the right to use classrooms for political activities by night and may even receive funding from the school.

High schools represent an important arena for youth parties. Every second year, a few weeks before the elections - elections are always held on the second Monday in September - all Norwegian high schools organise mock elections. All high school students vote during these elections, regardless of age, and the results are published a short time before the date of the elections. Although it does not count in the total score - high school students with the right to vote must still vote on the day of the elections - it is generally considered by politicians and the media to be a good indicator of the important trends in the campaign. In relation to these elections, all high schools organise public debates in front of all students where the different parties are invited to present their opinions on various issues. In these debates, one generally finds a mix of local, experienced politicians and people from the youth branches of the political parties.

These debates are often criticised for being superficial, populist and for lacking in gravity, but there is little doubt that they have a two major positive effects on youth parties. Firstly, youth parties have a unique opportunity to win new members as they travel across the country and meet all Norwegian high school students. It also means that most young people have an opportunity to meet people who are actively involved in youth politics, to ask questions, obtain information and eventually join an organisation if they wish to. Secondly, it means that young people who are already actively involved in party politics get a considerable amount of debating practice in front of people who are their own age or a little younger. There can be little doubt that such school debates serve as the main arena whereby young people can meet politicians and active youth party members. It provides an important point of entry into the school system, and thus into the lives of young people.

Membership of a youth political party is not limited to the elite. People involved in party politics come from a diverse array of social backgrounds, although young people whose parents have received an education, tend to be more highly represented. Like other youth organisations, youth parties can be a meeting place for people with different interests, backgrounds and with different objectives.

A high value-adding experience

Politics in general has much of the same status in Norway as in other countries. Surveys show that the confidence of people in politicians has diminished over time, and indeed, politicians are often made targets by people who complain that they do not talk the truth and do not keep their promises. But major scandals have been few in comparison with other European countries, and the perceived distance between politicians and the public is considerably lower than in, for example, France or Italy. It is my impression, having discussed the issue with young people from different European countries, that the political debate in Norway is reasonably close to the general public.

My personal involvement in party politics in Norway has left me with many positive experiences. A striking phenomenon was the challenging intellectual environment. I always felt that although I worked with people on the inside of one party, dissent and debate was not only tolerated but encouraged, discussion was frank, open and intellectually stimulating. The obligation to have an independent opinion on everything from Norway's membership in the European Union to local issues of property regulations, meant that I had a constant duty to pay attention to what was going on, and to think hard about my own views and ideas for the development of the society in which I live. In addition, the more general benefits of volunteer work were all part of the positive experience. The lessons I learned from organising meetings and seminars, debates and campaigns, working with teams of people from different backgrounds and of different ages have been extremely useful to me since.

Notes:

1.   Statistics Norway, www.ssb.no

How Old is Old Enough?
Campaigning to Lower the Voting Age

Matthew Green MP

Member of Parliament for Ludlow, and Liberal Democrat Spokesman on Young People, Education and Skills

Introduction

Along with the Citizenship Curriculum, the publication of the Electoral Commission's Consultation Paper, *How Old is Old Enough?* - the minimum age of voting and candidacy in UK elections, has pushed the campaign to lower the voting age to the top of the agenda. It is time to look again at the reasons why the voting age should be lowered, and it is time for these reasons to be acknowledged as valid. It is no longer good enough to merely say that young people don't want to vote, or cannot be trusted with major decisions. The hypocritical and under-developed counter-arguments which plague this issue should no longer be tolerated. If we are to ensure not only the survival, but the flourishing, of democracy and political engagement in this country, then we must ensure that the voting age is lowered to 16.

Young people are more cynical and less supportive of the political process in the first decade of the twenty-first century than young people in the 1990s were: consequently voter turnout among the young continues to fall. The question is: Do we chose to tackle this situation with radical reform of voting rights, or do we allow this disillusionment and disaffection to persist? Do we begin to allow our young people to face the responsibility of choosing their political representatives or do we allow them to become more cynical and sceptical because they have been excluded? Do we as a democratic and free country choose to promote democracy, or do we continue to maintain the status quo? Do we give our young people the chance to cast their vote - their stake in the future? After all, however flawed our democracy is, voting is our opportunity to mould the society in which we live.

The Votes at 16 Campaign is a campaign about these fundamental issues. It is about encouraging democracy and participation in the political process; but even more than that, it is about the fundamental issues of civil rights, respect and equality. The simple facts are: at present, 16 and 17 year olds can marry but are not trusted with the responsibility of casting a vote. 16 and 17 year olds in full-time work are expected to pay taxes but are not allowed to determine the politicians who raise them. And 16 and 17 year olds can die for their country serving in the armed forces, but cannot elect the Government which wages the war.

Promoting consistency

'Votes at 16' is about consistency. 16 and 17 year olds are treated by society as adults one minute and children the next. They are berated by society for lacking respect and responsibility, but are undermined by society's lack of trust in them. If young people are never given the power to determine their own destinies, then they will never be able to prove their ability to respect that responsibility. If we do not trust 16 and 17 year olds with the vote, then it should come as no surprise when they act irresponsibly. Where is their stake in the world? Where is their incentive to respect the society around them? Where is their voice: their say?

At a time when interest in politics among young people is low, the 'Votes at 16' campaign is an attempt to re-engage these young people. The increasing apathy towards politics, its institutions, its actors and its practices arises in some part from the fact that young people feel that they are so removed and alienated from the process. What is the point in younger teenagers discussing political issues and scrutinising political parties when they know that it is years before they will actually get a chance to influence the process? What is the point in young people trying to express their opinions to politicians who have little motivation to listen because they are not dependent on their votes? The democratic system is failing the young, and the consequences are despondency and disengagement from the political process.

Interest in Politics Wanes

There are some interesting facts, though, which demonstrate that this doesn't need to be the case. The estimated turnout at the 2001 General Election among 18-24 year olds was just 39%. This shows that by the time young people can vote they are already turned off by politics. Interestingly, though, an opinion poll carried out by Charter 88 and the YMCA following the 2001 General Election found that as many as 62% of 16 to 17-year-olds believed that voting was important. The research also showed that 61% of 16 to 17-year-olds believed that voting holds Government to account and 47% said that voting could have a lot of influence.

There is something of a difference between the opinions of 16 and 17 year olds in relation to politics and voting behaviour, and the actions of 18 to 24 year olds who actually have the right to vote. Most young people are interested in the society and world they live in - they are not born apathetic. However, enthusiasm for voting among younger teenagers diminishes over subsequent years. Research shows that as many as 47% of 16 to 17-year-olds said that voting could make a lot of difference - this drops to only 35% by the time they have reached their early twenties. By the age of 18, young people are often less idealistic, more disillusioned with the world, and consequently don't vote. There is a strong argument for engaging people at a younger age - at the age when their idealism and interest in the world is keener. It is at this age that the habit of voting should be instilled. After all, voting is a habit.

Developing responsibilty

The main arguments which are used to counter the 'Votes at 16' Campaign are that people under 18 are not sufficiently mature to use the right to vote properly; have insufficient understanding of the issues; are more likely to act irresponsibly and are more easily influenced by others. These arguments have never been rational or reasonable. Nowadays, however, in light of the introduction of compulsory Citizenship Education, these arguments appear even more flawed.

The Citizenship Curriculum is preparing young people better than ever before for using their vote. Citizenship Education teaches young people the ideas of social and moral responsibility, community involvement and nurtures and improves their political literacy. The fact is, however, by the time young people finish studying citizenship, at the age of sixteen, well-informed and engaged, they are denied the right to exercise this education. These young people are probably better informed and more able to cast their vote with a responsible, independent mind than many adults, yet we still deny them the right to express their opinions.

It is not only Citizenship Education which is preparing young people for political participation. There are now more student councils than ever before. Young people are encouraged to understand and take part in political processes in schools and colleges up and down the country. We are teaching our children to become active citizens, and encouraging them to express their views and learn to listen to others. This is hollow if young people feel that they are only trusted with these freedoms and responsibilities in only very limited situations.

The Electoral Commission's Consultation

The 'Votes at 16' Campaign has gathered huge momentum over the last few years. The campaign is supported by the Liberal Democrats, a huge number of political and non-governmental organisations, as well as the National Union of Students, Barnardo's, the Green Party, the YMCA, the Children's Society and London Young Labour. The Electoral Commission's consultation paper, How Old is Old Enough?, is a welcome and important step for the 'Votes at 16' campaign.

Pariahs or Midwives?
Youth Political Parties and British Political Culture

Elisabeth Rayment
Researcher at the New Politics Network

Youth political parties in Britain

F ew would deny that British political parties face challenges in raising, or even retaining their membership. In 1953 the Conservative party boasted a subscription of nearly three million and Labour of one million; today Conservative membership has plunged to under 300,000 and Labour to under 250,000. And this challenge is perhaps particularly clear for their youth wings. The Young Conservatives, who once counted a large slice of Middle England's young people among its members now have 10,000 in Conservative Future; there are an estimated 5000 members of Young Labour and around 2090 in the Liberal Democrat Youth and Students[1]. As Matt Henn and Mark Weinstein's research has demonstrated, young people are interested in political issues but perceive 'Politics' and political parties in particular to be largely irrelevant to their lives. And it seems that even where younger members are recruited, many leave soon after; in a recent article by the youth representative on Labour's National Executive Council, Jonny Reynolds, admitted that in Young Labour "retention rates are appalling, with most members bailing out after a year"[2].

The possibility of reducing the voting age from 18 to 16 provides some scope for increasing the participation of young people before they leave compulsory education. But it is equally important to look at attitudes to young people in political parties from the broader perspective of political culture. In doing so two questions must be answered. First, what role should youth wings play within the national parties? Second, where should political youth wings sit within the broad spectrum of youth organisations?

At present, the relationship between the youth wings of the main political parties and their central party hierarchies differs from party to party. Young

Labour and Conservative Future simply comprise those party members under the age of 26 and 30 respectively; though Conservative Future has a full-time staff member at Central Office and Young Labour does not, both are subsumed within the central structure. By contrast, as part of a federal party the LDYS is notionally separate from the other components, writing its own policies and with its own office. Nonetheless, in comparison with youth wings in other countries all the British parties are weak. In much of Europe party youth wings are separate organisations with a large staff and organisational network; the Young Democrats in Holland, for example, are recognised by D66 (Democrats of 66) but are otherwise separate.

The comparative weakness of British youth politics is also reflected in their funding. Of the three parties, the LDYS is unique in having a budget, funded by a membership rebate and a federal grant that totalled £37,800 in 2002 it is the only youth wing to declare its finances to the Electoral Commission. The finances of Conservative Future and Young Labour are more informal, a mixture of sponsorship and piecemeal grants from the party for specific projects. Project by project funding and an informal structure are not necessarily a disadvantage to a strong youth element in the parties. However, the comparative lack of paid staff and contingent finances place serious obstacles to the effective recruitment of young people, and thus ultimately to the presence of a vibrant youth wing. In his article for the Tribune Jonny Reynolds comments that:

> "[Labour] has never invested anything like the resources that a youth political organisation needs in order to undertake the most basic tasks."

The enthusiasm of young activists will only go so far; without the underpinning of resources and a commitment from the central party, recruitment among young people by young people will surely falter. If we are to take seriously the idea of encouraging young people to not just be informed but involved with political parties, a debate needs be held on the place of the younger members of political parties. Should youth wings be a separate structure from the central party? Should they have their own budget? Until these issues have been thought through the prospect of involving substantial numbers of young people in parties will remain simply an unfulfilled aspiration.

Engagement with youth organisations

Yet whatever the importance of the role of young people within political parties, the debate with the greatest implications for young people concerns the place of youth politics within the general sphere of youth organisations.

Unlike most youth organisations, the youth wings of political parties are not charities; even where they are notionally separate from the central party hierarchy, as in the case of the LDYS, they operate as unincorporated bodies governed by the party constitution. They are therefore excluded from most of the funding available to other youth organisations; many grants, including the National Lottery and the Neighbourhood Renewal Community Chest, are available only to 'charitable or benevolent' organisations. These restrictions ensure that the sources of funding for youth parties are comparatively small and narrow compared to other youth organisations, forcing them back on the generosity of the party.

However, the differences between youth parties and other youth organisations lie at a much more fundamental level than their legal or financial status. Indeed, at almost every point a clear distinction is drawn between youth organisations and youth political parties. In this climate a lack of access to grants is only symptomatic of the wider dichotomy between youth politics and other youth organisations.

Indeed it is widely accepted that political parties should be excluded from initiatives involving young people. The UK Youth Parliament, an organisation designed to give young people a voice and model the British democratic process, bars the election of representatives connected to political parties. The National Youth Agency, an organisation working "to advance youth work to promote young people's personal and social development and their voice, influence and place in society" holds no information on the youth wings of political parties; the British Youth Council, "run for and by young people representing their views to central and local government" is virtually unique in allowing the affiliation of party youth wings. This is again reflected back in eligibility for grants. Coming under the auspices of the Department for Education and Skills, the policy of the Local Network Fund for Children and Young People "enabling voluntary and community groups to provide local solutions to poverty and social exclusion" has a particular clause barring organisations that promote political beliefs. The government's Community Champions Fund, seeking to "develop the work of local people in changing their communities for the better" has activities of "a political or predominantly religious nature" at the top of its list of those not suitable to be supported. Likewise, Millennium Volunteers, a scheme encouraging young people to play a part in their community, operates projects ranging from youth councils to sports clubs but bars volunteering with political organisations.

This distinction between youth work and youth politics holds too for the involvement of political parties in schools. The understandable concern among some teachers to maintain their own neutrality has often led to a vacuum of information on the parties, and despite the element of political education in citizenship the presence of the parties in schools remains minimal. A nationwide project to see MPs visit local secondary schools, launched in July 2002 by the Hansard Society, is a significant step forward, but the 1500 schools who have asked for resource packs represent only a minority of secondary educators. The idea that young people could themselves represent the views of their party to their peers, a commonplace in Norway, is virtually unheard of in Britain. Moreover, these disparities in the treatment of youth political wings and youth organisations are only a reflection of a widespread attitude towards politics, an attitude that treats the parties, especially when dealing with young people, with distinct unease and even suspicion. A concerned youth worker was surely not alone when he commented that he did not want "his" young people to "fall into the clutches of politicians".

Challenging the youth work / youth political distinction

The distinction between youth work and youth politics is so deeply engrained that it is rarely challenged. But is it justified? Are party political youth wings really so different from other youth organisations? There are of course complexities in dealing with political parties and their involvement with young people. Young people must not be exploited: no-one wants to see young people brainwashed into slavish devotion to any one party. It is also right that we broaden our notion of the political. Politics is clearly more than parties, and a group of young people pressing their local council to clear up their local park should be recognised as a political act. But even with these caveats in place there is ample room to challenge the existing polarisation of youth political parties and other youth organisations.

First, although politics must mean more than just the parties, they are still the fundamental unit of our political culture and should be correspondingly important. Recent research has consistently demonstrated that participation in elections correlates with party identification; the 2001 British Social Attitudes survey, for example, revealed that only 28% of those who had no party identification voted, in contrast to the 89% with very strong allegiance to a party. If young people rarely come across political parties at their own local level and if we do not encourage them to become involved, even informally, we cannot expect participation in elections among first time voters to rise.

Second, by dividing political parties from youth organisations we risk incoherence in our strategy to increase the participation of young people in society. Rightly jarred by the staggeringly low turnout among young people at the 2001 election, the government has poured money into initiatives to encourage young people to participate in their local community. And many of these projects have been very successful. Involving many projects that affect young people, the Community Champions Fund has been worth £9 million over three years and hopes to make 260 Champion awards in the coming year, for example. But if these initiatives are never connected to the party political system, Britain's chief forum for debate and change, we will only perpetuate the suspicion that political parties are remote and irrelevant, that they are only a necessary evil from which young people must be protected. Without a reassessment of how this gulf between parties and projects can be bridged, the involvement of young people in political parties will remain an unrealised and distant ambition.

A way forward?

So what can be done? In the short term the political parties could be persuaded to fund their youth wings more generously: national staff workers would certainly increase the effectiveness of recruitment practices. In the longer term, a potential solution lies in the public funding of youth political parties, as in Norway and funding bodies could also be encouraged to consider opening their grants to youth wings. From the perspective of community involvement, funding could be made available to youth political groups for projects connected to civic engagement. The Electoral Commission's New Initiatives Fund, for example, launched in 2002 to "promote engagement with democratic processes and elections' does not preclude applications from political parties, providing that they do not use the fund to promote their own views. It would thus be possible for youth wings to be funded to go into schools to discuss elections and encourage young people to participate.

Yet these are only first steps. Jonny Reynolds is right, and speaks for more than just his own party, when he comments that:

> "a properly staffed and resourced youth organisation is not an optional extra, but integral to the party's future success"

But surely we need to go much further than this? The treatment of political youth wings and their uneasy relationship with other youth organisations is an issue that transcends debates over whether political parties should be represented at the UK Youth Parliament or bid for a DfES grant. At its heart lies the question of the very role that political parties should play in modern British society. And we need to challenge at all levels the increasingly negative attitudes towards the parties; until an alternative is found they remain our means of changing the government, the linchpin of our democracy. Politicians must work to see more effective representation, to present their policies to young people with integrity and to genuinely care about their views. But voters too must see that to stand outside of the political parties is, whether we like them or not, to stand outside of the political system. The long-term risks for our democracy would suggest that this is something we must seek to prevent among young people, however high the cost.

Pariahs or Midwives?

Notes

1. Source: David Pugh, Conservative Future; Liberal Democrat Membership Department
2. Age Time Bomb Ready to Explode, Tribune, 18 July 2003, p28

Afterword

Afterword
The Broader Context

Sir Bernard Crick

Emeritus Professor of Politics, Birkbeck College, University of London, and adviser on citizenship to the DfES 1998-2000

"I have sought to build on my previous policy thinking to outline a clear framework for civil renewal – one that can give definition and purpose to the next wave of government reform. […] Terms such as 'civil renewal' and 'active citizenship' may conjure up images of do-gooding or sitting in endless local meetings […] but whatever the terminology, the crucial policy imperatives are clear. We must aim to build strong, empowered and active communities, in which people increasingly do things for themselves and the state acts to facilitate, support and enable citizens to lead self-determined, fulfilled lives. In this way, we will genuinely link the economic and social, the civil and formal political arena, the personal with the public realm."

Rt. Hon. David Blunkett MP.
The CSV Edith Kahn Memorial Lecture.[1]

The contributions in this collection of essays show the vigour, width and the rigour of the citizenship movement. There can be no doubts on that score. Some real differences in content and method, yes, even different agendas, but there is room for varying emphasis within the broad headings of the Citizenship Curriculum in England and the somewhat similar advisory proposals in Scotland. The National Curriculum Order is expressed far more briefly than any other, deliberately to leave a now unusual degree of freedom to both teachers and taught. David Blunkett described the Order as a "light touch" and I, perversely, called it "strong bare bones".

The doubts which exist, should not be with the intention, the curriculum or the dedication and skills within what I still call the citizenship movement[2], but rather with the implementation of the subject. The Ofsted report on the first year of implementation does show worrying signs in some schools: an over-emphasis on the knowledge-based part of the curriculum, a retreat into something like old Civics; a nervousness about holding discussions on real issues; a lack of preparation and in-service training; and a widespread confusion of Citizenship with PSHE, often due to head teachers somewhat thoughtlessly taking the line of least resistance and allocating special responsibility to the head of PSHE - who is sometimes the arms, legs and whole body as well. Now of course there is PSHE and PSHE. The worry about this marriage, whether shot-gun or of love and mutual understanding, is that it can sometimes marginalise the political literacy part of the curricular triad (social and moral, community and political literacy). More generally – once again – good citizenship and good behaviour can avoid the more risky company of active citizenship.

The Preface to this collection of essays quotes me as saying - at some meeting, unaware that press were present:

> "I may be father of the movement, but I will strangle the child if it's just a bloody waste of time".

I may well have been quoted accurately. Certainly I had in mind that the curriculum was already overloaded. Even if some schools are over-obsessed with targets, there is good evidence - *vide* Derry Hannam's contribution - that more participative schools do not suffer in the league tables. Indeed some, by giving a sense of possession to the young - 'our school!' - can motivate them to do well in all or most other subjects. Most of all I had in mind that the DfES had funded an eight-year large-scale longitudinal study[3] to see what changes occur in knowledge, attitudes and participative behaviour.

A national need and a long-term government policy

It is only responsible that there should be a terminal judgement, and that interim reports create an opportunity to trim, adjust and reform, if necessary. The National Curriculum is not frozen. The coming of Citizenship showed that. Citizenship itself cannot be frozen. This is worrying to some teachers but attractive to others. "Light touch" allows for improvements and running repairs rather than a false sense of certainty. I had a small political motive in pressing for the large expenditure on the longitudinal study - money which could, of course, have been well spent elsewhere. It was a sign that government meant to stick with Citizenship, and was not, as some journalists thought, an obsession of Blunkett's that would wither on the vine on his departure. This was a national need and a long-term government policy. Precisely because, as some critics say, this innovation is "a piece of social engineering", that we need reasonably objective measures to see whether it works.

The present ministerial team have made good and understanding speeches about the need to promote active citizenship. The Preface is right to say that the introduction of Citizenship "ranks among the boldest changes to secondary education implemented by the present government", but the Preface is also right to hint that if it stands alone simply as a new subject, like any other, it is unlikely to alter the culture of a school, let alone of the country; right, too, to hint that there has been a certain quietness about the whole matter both in government and the media. For that we should, on the whole, be devoutly thankful. Great care was taken to offer few hazards to fortune: the whole thing could have been denounced as "New Labour indoctrination"[4]. Not merely the good sense of David Blunkett prevented this, but the active support of Kenneth (Lord) Baker who served on the advisory group - telling us that he had wanted it as part of his national curriculum, but that she had said "no", and now the sympathetic tolerance of Damian Green at the time of implementation last September. If good and active citizenship could have been a natural for the Prime Minister's vision or search for 'a Third Way'[5], perhaps a certain nervousness about possible media reaction came from advisers in No 10, or perhaps a prudence that claiming it as "among the boldest changes" might provoke instant opposition – I mean provoke the Opposition instantly.

Some ministers do say that Citizenship in schools should help remedy the low youth vote and widespread disinterest in or cynicism about politics and politicians. Well, it may be able to help a bit, if a school has built up a habit of discussion and voting on issues real to the kids; but it is unfair and unrealistic to saddle schools with all that responsibility. I take a commonsense view that the example set by those in public life, and the conduct of government and clarity of policies, are far more influential stimulants or deterrents. Lowering the voting age to sixteen can be argued as a matter of right, but it will make little difference to turnout unless national politics changes its recent character.

If, however, there is some disappointment in the citizenship movement about a relative quietness on high, it could be said that a good deal of good is being done by stealth, as it were – rather like the media's view of Gordon Brown's redistribution policies through the intricacies of indirect taxation.

In 1997 New Labour established an Active Community Unit in the Home Office. It its fair to say that, after the press release, there was a certain lack of leadership or sense of direction in - or not accorded to - that fairly large unit. But when Blunkett became Home Secretary the inactive Community Unit became active. The advertisement for the post of head of the unit was for someone from the voluntary sector, experienced in both hands-on and administration. The head of NACRO was appointed, someone who had spent half her time applying for Home Office funding and the other half fighting them over policy. The unit has embarked on an ambitious programme of support for community groups, including a programme - pilots for which begin shortly - of citizenship education for community leaders and activists.

The 2002 Nationality, Immigration and Asylum Act requires residents in the United Kingdom seeking British citizenship (i.e. naturalisation) to show "a sufficient knowledge of English, Welsh or Scottish Gaelic" and to have "a sufficient knowledge about life in the United Kingdom". The independent advisory group[6] not surprisingly interpreted "Life in the United Kingdom" to include a substantial element of knowledge about political, legal and social institutions, and also positive incentives for those with reasonable English already to provide a profile of civic involvement or volunteering as part of the requirement.

The Neighbourhood Renewal Unit in the Deputy Prime Minister's department concentrates funding on the eighty-four most deprived areas in the country, and its remit not merely enjoins consultation with those affected but also training for local groups. The new system of public consultative committees in the NHS similarly offers, indeed requires, some training in citizenship skills - information retrieval and advocacy - as well as specific knowledge of the Health Service. The Home Office's Active Community Unit has been designated by the Treasury as the lead department to produce a cross-government coordinated programme for training in citizenship and community leadership skills. There are, of course, the thirty 16-19 pilot schemes for citizenship - funded by DfES and run by the LSDA - each designed to bring Further Education Colleges or Sixth Forms into an active collaboration with national and local voluntary bodies in a mixture of class-room based learning and learning in the community. One hopes that these pilots will fly and cover all the ground. A decision cannot be delayed long.

The meaning of citizenship

Confusion does remain, however, on what is meant by citizenship. An Ofstead inspector came to an FE college where a lecturer was proud to tell that his lads had organised a party in an old people's home all by themselves. They had taken care to find what kind of food and music the old people would actually like. On inquiry, the inspector discovered that there had been no preparatory teaching on what is admittedly one of the most difficult problems in the country, the interface between the personal social services and the health services – why were some of the old people in a 'home' at all, rather than being cared for at home? What were supposed to be the demarcation lines, and the national and local policies governing these cases? What safe-guards and arrangements for inspection? Had there not been some recent reports on abuses? Did they think things could be improved? None of this had been raised in class, before or after. The inspector asked a group of consultants to the 16-19 projects if they thought this was what was wanted. There was a general shaking of heads. That was good citizenship, indeed, but not active citizenship. True citizenship is working together with others to effect or resist change.

Notes:

1.   June 11, 2003, Published by Home Office Communication Directorate, 2003.
2.   Which now includes a new, rapidly growing and officially recognised Association for Citizenship Teaching
3.   Conducted by the NFER, advised by David Kerr
4.   Despite there being some difficulty with calling the chairman of the advisory group 'New Labour'
5.   I was once warned by a minister not to repeat my joke "since we no longer believe in socialism, we might as well believe in democracy"
6   Who reported on September 4 as The New and the Old